THE SAD DEMISE OF HENRY

AND OTHER KEY WEST MUSINGS

THE SAD DEMISE OF HENRY
AND OTHER
KEY WEST MUSINGS

Jack Mazur

ABSOLUTELY AMAZING eBOOKS

ABSOLUTELY AMAZING eBOOKS

Published by Whiz Bang LLC, 926 Truman Avenue, Key West, Florida 33040, USA.

For information contact:
Publisher@AbsolutelyAmazingEbooks.com

ISBN-13: 978-1508871897
ISBN-10: 1508871892

THE SAD DEMISE OF HENRY

AND OTHER KEY WEST MUSINGS

CONTENTS

THE SAD DEMISE OF HENRY

On October 29th, 2008, Henry, a rooster of indeterminate origin and a resident of Key West, was found dead just off Little Lane in a driveway by a woman from across the street.

A lively creature in his prime he stood his ground amidst the tourists, even the naked and drunk ones and let everyone know he was there. A rooster makes noise. They are the tea party newcomers of Key West and cluck and strut in their own self-importance. Sally Mae Hutchinson, a relatively recent arrival from another island habitat observed as Henry was slowly and unmethodically erased from the census of the living breathing poultry population. She did nothing about it and went about her business in the yard next door.

It was a driver with Pennsylvania plates recently placated by the wares available on Duval Street that did the dirty deed. He was henpecked, as it were, by his girlfriend and showing all the negative attributes she had learned from a double crossed Catholic mother up north. Henry had no Catholic mother. He was a chicken. He was found dead in the driveway at somewhere around noon on the aforementioned day. He had been run over repeatedly as the driver and his girlfriend argued over whether to attend a sex club or munch on conch fritters on a local dock.

After their eventual departure and murderous behavior Jeffrey, the caretaker of the "Delighthouse," appeared in the driveway and upon espying the carcass of the recently departed obtained a shovel and unceremoniously chucked Henry over the chain length fence into the yard of Sally Mae. This particular caretaker had been convicted and served a sizable portion of his life in prison for a set of serial killings in the early 1970s. He had been released partially for good behavior but also because of the overcrowding caused by the internment of thousands of child support cheats. A dead body, any dead body meant nothing to him. Keeping his job and therefore the driveway clean did.

The next morning Sally Mae was having her coffee when her neighbor dropped by to let her know that there was a dead chicken just inside her fence. This was no uncommon occurrence. Where ever there are live chickens there are bound to be dead ones. In Sally Mae's opinion if it were a domesticated chicken it would be a cooked chicken. But it wasn't and so Sally Mae took her ten-foot stick with its forked end and removed Henry from her yard by depositing him back onto the driveway of the "Delighthouse." Thus began the Key West version of the chicken-tossing Hatfields and McCoys.

Henry and I had met in a segregated dining room in a Woolworth's in Wilmington, Delaware back in 1967. He was a pretty good chicken as roosters go. Maybe a little loud mouthed and prone to sticking out his chest around 5 am no matter the day. We were both drafted into the army that year and somehow ended up in the same dining room during a weekend pass. We weren't supposed to eat together as per Jim Crow laws of the time but we did anyway and no one seemed to care all that much due to the relative latitude of Delaware on the map. I remember that Henry had problems with uniform fittings. I also remember that he was more than a little miffed that I made E-2 before he did. Henry went to Viet Nam and served on some weird Army riverboats. I went to Germany and partied every night. All I could think of at the time was that Viet Nam was a poor place to be a chicken.

We once met up on leave in Oakland. I was on my way to Nam and he was on his way back. I still remember the locals throwing corn at him and calling him baby killer. He was a staff sergeant at the time. He had the far away look that is so over used as descriptive by journalists and novelists. He did his time and his duty and after we had a few beers I never saw him again.

What next happened to Henry was that his world depreciated and he fell into extremely bad times. He migrated across the country, played guitar in a few bands and sang with a guy that promulgated boat drinks and hanging out in flip flops. He started snorting cocaine and smoking bales of pot. Henry ended up on the wrong side of the fence as far as nice society goes. He traveled south picking tomatoes and filleting fish until one day he found himself on the doorstep of the Florida Keys. The weather was warm and the drugs were easy to obtain. He slept in the mangroves and the occasional abandoned boat. He took a mistress and conceived a complete henhouse of his progeny. His family is well-known in parts of Bahama

Village. He quit drugs but would take two glasses of Merlot each day about sundown. He became fond of Cuban cigars and through connections always had a supply to dole out to friends and acquaintances.

One day his life was snuffed out by a careless and non-caring northerner on Little Street just a few days before Halloween. Sally Mae and the caretaker serial killer tossed his body over the fence for about three days until another northerner took the time to explain to Jeffrey that what he was doing was un-Christian. Jeffrey thought for a moment and tossed him over the fence. Henry was finally laid to rest on Sally Mae's property on the first of November, 2008. These days I sometimes sit on a friend's porch on the second floor and look out over Little Street where Henry lived his last days. I think of the times I spent with him, talking to him and commiserating about life. He was a good American and a combat veteran. Things are sometimes better elsewhere. He has crossed over. I wish him peace.

THE BRIDGE

In my experience there's always a need to get away.

Although I have gotten away by moving myself to the Florida Keys I still have the need to get away from my house, my housemates, the television and electronic devices. Luckily, one day while driving around aimlessly, I found a place to position myself in contemplative repose. It's a place that I always bring my fishing rod to along with a twelve pack of beer steeped in ice. It's a bridge at the end of my island habitat that leads nowhere yet offers me the silence and quietude that I've always struggled to find.

Almost every morning I've gotten in the truck with fishing pole and bait, or lately a lure to while away my time while figuring out the universe's problems. At this stage I may have figured them out but I haven't solved a one. If I did solve a problem who would I tell? I'm not well connected with governments or religions. Maybe it's just as well as my solutions may not be practical or cost effective or mean anything at all to those who claim to be in charge. There certainly seems to be a lot of people claiming to be in charge. As I stand on the bridge completely alone with a southeasterly breeze and a line in the water I ask: "in charge of what?"

Some days I reflect on past romances. Where are these women now? What have I done to them to make them forego my presence? What overindulgence or body odor or mislaid phrase put me into a position of yearning for what

I had only yesterday? There's no answer to this. Women have their emotional cocoons that can only be breached with a certain kind of permission. I respect and admire the type of man that can understand this debacle and knows how to move forward. Sadly I don't have the tools. As there is a tug on the line and I'm using bait I reel in a small mangrove snapper. Not much of a fun catches but a fish nonetheless. I notice the parallels to my thoughts. I wonder how far down the list I may have been to someone's ego. I wonder if it disturbed them to 'scttle.'

Some days I just stand on the bridge shirtless and absorb the sun. The repetition of sunny days has turned my skin golden brown and my hair, although basically gray, to blonde. This is good for my self-esteem only because it makes me think that I'm desirable. To look in the mirror I have to face the fact that I'm 58 years old. Desirability as per appearances is on the downslide. The fact is that to attract I must be outgoing, sociable and willing to accept other opinions and points of view. And I should probably do this with a few less beers in evidence. As I look into the crystal water below I see several tarpon and I wonder what it would be like to hook one. If Hemingway enjoyed the large fish encounter why shouldn't I? Contemplation be damned!

On other days I'm using a lure and thinking about the horrible terrorist that was just taken down. How can someone hate someone else so much? How can someone with so much wealth and privilege decide to live like a dog and vow to kill my countrymen and Christians any and everywhere? I'm fishing for barracuda because I'm looking for a fight. The snappers are fine but I want something to yank the line almost out of my hands. Again the man from Whitehead Street is showing me that fishing is the noble art of the hunter and the hunted and no one has a particular edge despite science and the march of time. The tug on the line comes and as I peer into the water I see the largest fish that has ever bitten onto one of my lines. Since he's already in shallow clear water I watch the complete undirected scene. It's an 85-pound tarpon that's taken the lure and he makes his first jump from the water. I've only seen bass jump from fresh water ponds on television fishing shows. But I consider what I've seen to be magnificent! There's always a bend to the fish, his gills are always glaring, his determination to get free is ever-present. And sometimes he does. Then you make the probable deduction that the fish is at least as smart as your last girlfriend. My fish jumped three times and I was as proud as any character written about in novels about Caribbean fishermen. Majesty! Majesty was before me and took me from my reverie and jolted me from my stoic thoughts on a bridge in the middle of nowhere. The line snapped as that point. Another one that got away. I didn't mind so much because of the rush of the near miracle and the thought that, for once, I used the right bait.

Some days on the bridge the Navy fighter pilots come over in their F-15s and F-16s. They come out of Boca Chica and fly in razor thin closeness. You hear them before they come and they are louder after they're gone. The best friend of my life, a big brother type, and a Navy fighter pilot died in 1972 in a head on collision with another fighter jet during maneuvers in the Atlantic. I often thought that he made a massive cover-up just to see if I would make something out of myself. That was youthful thinking. He's dead. And that's life.

But the fighter jets make me feel protected. As a Navy veteran I can see what they are doing are advanced maneuvers. The wings are loaded with weaponry and they mean business. Most of what they do is practice while their aircraft carriers spend a little R and R stateside. But the other part of what they do is protect our southernmost border. About a dozen jets scare the shit out of Cuba. There's also sub-chasers that stay in the sky for up to 20 hours. These are big lumbering craft with the sonar tail, the four engines and one must think a crew of twelve. Some days the SEALS are practicing about two miles out. They jump from Apaches and get picked up again. I reel in the line to find a stupid ass blowfish on the end. I see an iguana in its fast paced waddle cross the road. There's an osprey eying my lure and I hope I don't have to deal with that. The SEALS fly away. Maybe its time for the mancave!

Under my house, built on 14 ten foot pillars, there is a concrete area that I've set up with a concrete table, some chairs, bawdy electric lights, painted tin lizards from the Christmas Tree Shoppe and excessive flotsam and jetsam; I have a space, like many, called the mancave. It is strictly for drinking beer and staring off into space for ten hours a day. Absolutely nothing gets done here. I tell myself that, yes, it actually does but one of those other mind compartments shouts out the obvious truth! I'm a useless lazy shit some days. From there I venture out onto the dock and Tiki Hut. The temperature is overwhelmingly excessive. I give it ten minutes, jump into the canal, and them I'm out. I change into the other pair of "dry" shorts that are always on the back of a chair somewhere. I sit, crack a beer and think of other useless detritus.

While on the bridge I'm usually in the middle, if not off to one side. It sounds so obvious but there are different sides and even different middles. Is this bridge for fishing? Is this bridge a continuation of a road? Again, so obvious. I'm gonna go over to the far side now and I guess I'll just follow the signs. And just as I was leaving another stinkin' rotten blowfish grabs on my line and makes me linger about 20 feet above the beginning of the channel only 90 miles from the Port of Havana!

BLUEGRASS BEACH BUM

Randy wanted to see all his bluegrass friends and maybe pick a little guitar. The only problem that swerved over the yellow line was that he was in Key West. And that didn't suck!

Randy spent a lot of time fishing. He fished bridges, canals, beaches and sometimes got invited on a boat. He didn't know all that much about it but he did know that it was fun and relaxing. All of the world's problems dissipated as soon as he got his fishing rod out of the back of his beat up car. There was no woman telling him the direction his life should go. There wasn't a boss giving him a semi-annual performance review. He had a little money and a place to live. He had a cooler iced up with his favorite beer and the Florida Straits stretched out before him. And the sun warmed his barely clothed body so that he turned the color of molasses topped cornbread.

Sometimes he thought of the fishes below and which species might bite on his hook today. Other times he replayed some long lost sexual fantasy in his head. He had shed himself from the implanted Baptist guilt that he grew up with and took himself back to his 20s and 30s when fishing for fish was very far from his mind. In his mind he had done okay. He had been very lucky in the lust department and had never been married nor had ever had children.

That's where his reverie had taken him when he became aware of the three Haitians in the world's worst looking open boat. It was about ten feet long and had an outboard motor but it wasn't working. Randy didn't know they were Haitians at first until they started yelling at him in French. He disengaged, as it were, from the college coed he had been romancing and tried to focus on his new company. This was his free time with nature and initially he wasn't pleased. The extremely sincere pleading of the three men in the boat brought him to his senses. He didn't know how they got there. He had been fishing, staring at the Florida Straits and making love to someone whose name he had forgotten. But, not any more.

On the left side of the bridge where he usually fished there was a boat launch below. He made hand signals to the three that they should endeavor to land on that spot. Because Randy had spent over a year in France he knew how to find a bathroom, order a croissant and ask for a "blond bier." He went down the embankment to the boat launch to assess the situation. It was fairly apparent that the three men in the boat weren't looking for croissants or were in any great need for a bathroom. So he offered them some beer. He never made friends so fast!

He indicated to all three that to get out of the boat they had to be careful as the boat launch was covered in a slime that grew during high tide, which apparently, during his mental sexcapade, had occurred. He didn't speak French, they wanted the American Dream. All three were on their asses inside of ten seconds. It really was funny and they were quite proud and happy to be on American soil. The four of them made it up to the beach in various stages of euphoria and success.

That's when the expensive black SUV drove up to the edge of the beach. An older white guy got out of the vehicle and he was immediately identifiable. He had a blue baseball cap and strands of what was left of his former blond hair. There was a time when Randy would have liked meeting him. This wasn't the day. He had seen the watery acrobatics and the loss of beer from the road. He went to his car and pulled four waters from his cooler right after he made a quick phone call. He came back over and tried to make sure everyone was all right. Indeed everyone was all right and there seemed to be true wonderment and thankfulness all around. The world is sometimes just a beautiful place to exist. An iguana crossed the road. A pelican splashed into the canal under the bridge.

It was with some disappointment that Randy noticed another vehicle coming to stop on the road. Four agents from Immigration and Naturalization approached them and two had weapons drawn. In this out of the way spot there was no place for the Haitians to run even if they were in shape to do so. The agents and the Haitians were gone within five minutes all within the vehicle recently arrived with the boaters and agents separated by metal mesh. Before they left the older guy that had showed up went over to the vehicle and gave the three Haitians a copy each of his new CD.

That moment in time was always condensed in Randy's mind. These poor men who had challenged the Caribbean in a small boat without enough gas had been defeated in their efforts. As Randy later told it while picking with a bunch of friends at the Grey Fox Bluegrass Fest he punched the older guy in the nose and watched him fall to the ground. As the blood gushed from the wound the old guy asked, "What'd you do that for?" Randy responded that he once bought a hamburger at this guy's restaurant and had to pay $20 for it. And on top of that it's the only place in Key West where you can't smoke!

Randy drives an eighteen-wheeler now for the same dude and has to watch at every gig how all the participants are dressed up in all kindsa rubber inner tubes, parrot feathers and ugly shirts. But he always remembered the punch. And, boy, could he play, 'Long Black Veil'!

COCONUT TELEGRAPH

I got the call on a Thursday or Friday noon. Can't remember which and as with most things in Key West it wasn't important.

But I was on the road within the half hour and heading into Weirdville. The great Jimmy Buffett was playing unannounced on Duval Street at three. Big whup! After the last several books that I wrongly purchased I felt that the Hero was bragging a bit about his worldly goods. Airplanes, six or seven houses, GPS systems, fishing rods, trips to Montana, newly opened restaurants. I had a burger in Margaritaville in Key Weird. Cost me twenty bucks with no side orders. Couldn't smoke either. Can't smoke in Outlawville? Gimme a break. You can smoke in church in Key West!

I checked in with my friend Flo over by the lighthouse. While parking the car I couldn't stop thinking about my friend Henry the recently departed rooster. He lived by the lighthouse. He crowed at two in the afternoon over by the lighthouse. Fucking lunatic! I miss the bastard. Flo had one rolled and we partook amidst the blue smoke and the noise of the jets on their approach to the airport. Henry's relatives crowed for no particular reason. It was good enough reason to get out on the streets.

The Parrotheads were having their annual meeting of the minds and they were everywhere. The nice thing I can say about them is that they are extremely laid back. The not so nice thing is that they have obviously gained some weight over the years. Well, so have I. Live and let live. Flo and I headed over to Duval. Of course I stepped in some chicken shit. Henry's kids! I wiped it off on a rented red Mustang convertible. I felt immediately better.

Out on Duval the throng was growing like an excited male member. I knew that the Coral Reefer Band would be present and that Jimmy was just a rumor. The crowd that met me at Southard voided all that. Parrotheads to the left and Parrotheads to the right. Parrotheads on the balconies and Parrotheads on the roofs. There were a lot of Parrotheads. Within five minutes there was the great man himself on stage, live and looking extremely wealthy. Why didn't I think up that beach bum life, with a tan, middlin' guitar playin' and a laid-back attitude. BECAUSE I'm stupid! You know what he's got better than me? Teeth! He's got better teeth. Millionaires get that.

Flo wants to go up front. I haven't been to a rock concert (c'mon it's a rock concert) since the Eagles in 1977. And that's because crowds suck. They push and shove and do stupid things and smell badly and someone always has an M-80 they want to light off. Once at a Dead concert in Springfield, Mass I was hit in the head with a ham sub with lettuce tomato and mayo and I wasn't even hungry. Then the M-80 went off! The mayo saved my hearing. I chucked the tomato into the crowd on general principals. Felt kinda good about it too!

So Flo is dragging me thru the crowd and it gets more and more crowded in the crowd. The crowd is very crowdy. And there's lotsa people, too! We meander and push and squirm toward the front. Wuzzat smell? I don't know what it is for sure but something smells. It occurs to me suddenly that all of these Parrotheads decided against a shower this morning. I'm being crushed from behind. The liver and onions and corned beef and cabbage has congealed in the area where I'm standing. I wanna toss out buckets of Right Guard or Shower to Shower but I have none. I smell good. Why can't all these laid-back Parrotheads with boatdrinks in tow smell the same? If I had some garlic, hot sauce, and some oregano I could make gumbo right here! Just have to steal some celery out of some of the Bloody Marys.

We're near the front. The Great One is playing songs I never heard of but the Parrotheads are all singing along. Probably learned all the songs from the stereo in their summer homes on the cape or their yachts while sailing down the Intercoastal. Apparently neither the yachts or summer homes had running water, soap or shampoo! But hey, it's Jimmy Buffett. Flo continues to the front. I'm being pushed forward as if there was actually more room up there to stand around in. There's enough room to pee on your own foot. Maybe that was what was happening. I'm retreating like the allies at the Battle of the Bulge in December, 1944. Those allies smelled better than the Parrotheads surrounding me. I head off to the rear and listen for a while. Its much more comfortable here. Hey, here's a song I've heard of before. I'm in a groove. Everything smells better. Man, that Buffett sure is in good shape. This isn't me. I head off to Bob-a-lu's to get a cocktail and wait for Flo. Lookin' for my lost shaker of salt.

. . . AND STUFF.

I'm hitting flies with a rolled up newspaper until the air conditioner gets in its groove and makes all the bastards a little lethargic.

Then my ex-landlord calls and asks if I want to go to church with him. This is an easy answer. But then he says this is a different church and they aren't pushy and don't stomp their feet and point Jesus at you like a weapon. The answer isn't going to change. Then he says that everyone is seated cafe style like in a restaurant and they serve scrambled eggs, toast, grits and home fries. The choral is all electric rock music in a laid-back style kinda like the Eagles singing about redemption. Scrambled eggs AND grits? Well, I AM a Christian.

Then I got to thinking about that sect of Baptists out in Kentucky and western North Carolina that worship rattlesnakes. They've got rattlesnakes crawling all over themselves and they're like dance partners from God! They're not gonna bite you, no. Not unless you're a doubting Thomas. Then they'll plug your ass so quick! Snakes are favored in the Bible. If a snake thinks yer a cheat then by God yer a cheat! And iffin yer a cheat why would you wake up one particular morning and decide to go down to the church and let a rattlesnake bite yer ass or face? Do you really think a rattlesnake knows your heart? Well, maybe the ones in North Carolina.

So after thinking it over with all the rattlesnake venom versus the scrambled eggs and grits (with home fries and toast) and nobody pushing me to walk up front and confess all my sins to the whole congregation I'm thinkin' that the next time my ex-landlord invites me to church I owe it to myself to attend. In my best pressed Hawaiian shirt!

Amongst the Conchs down here (old time Key Westers) it seems every sentence ends with...and stuff! "...and stuff!" I took a heady crap and ran out of toilet paper...and stuff. This world's going to hell in a hand basket...and stuff. Would you like to sleep with me ... and stuff? All in all I'm steering away from the rattlesnakes and heading towards the scrambled eggs and grits...and stuff!

CUBANS, A BLACK TAHOE, AND A TALL TALE

It was just me and the Cubans fishing off the bridge one day recently. Exploring tourists would drive up on the bridge and ask if we caught anything. They thought it was friendly. I thought it was interference in my meditation. I already had to listen to too loud Spanish coming from four different mouths concerning what I'll never know and just prattlin' on about any little thing. If Castro had been just a little bit friendlier to these people I could have been fishing alone. Like God intended. It's me and a fishing pole. Who needs international politics?

Finally the Cubans caught enough 7-inch mangrove snapper to have a good fried supper and went on their way. Of course they turned up the stereo in their car and listened to that Calypso soul music they can't live without at a decibel level equal to a space shuttle lift off. Could still hear 'em five miles off! Then it's me, some mangroves and the Florida Straits. My mind wants to have fun with me and it reminds that the dudes I saw on Duval last night sure weren't Florida Straights. Nice skirts, though. And, yes Margaret, you CAN drink too much beer! As long as there is a man standing and who wants to maintain the image quintessential to the steadfast nature of...of...okay brain, you can turn that crap off.

From over a mile away I can always hear the tires on the pavement of approaching vehicles. It's not like waiting for Santa Claus. I've got a 50/50 chance someone is gonna ask me if the fish are biting or did I catch anything or where does this road go? Mr. Brain has all these smartass answers I can deliver and some are so intense that it would take a Bodhisattva to figure out. Don't run into those every day says the brain. "Yeah, I know," I say out loud. Stupid brain.

Then it arrives. A black Chevy Tahoe with tinted windows and built like it's going to survive a nuclear explosion. The electric window comes down as the vehicle comes to a stop. A pair of aviator sunglasses asks, "Catch anything?" Of course Mr. Brain has answers, solutions, comebacks, wisecracks, you name it but I squeeze his larynx. "No," I say. "That misses the point." A back window comes down and another pair of aviator glasses with a kind of high-pitched pseudo Southern accent asks, "Y'all want a beer?". This is weird but yeah I DO want a beer since mine are in my cooler a hundred yards away in my car. The driver turns off the ignition right there on the bridge and before Mr. Brain can even evaluate the situation there's four Aviator sunglasses dancing around me setting up tables, unfolding chairs, spreading out tablecloths and pulling fried chicken and potato salad from out of their asses. I'm asked to take a seat and for once Mr. Brain isn't sending or receiving any signals. The last guy out of the car is the guy who asked if I wanted a beer. He's got a six-pack in his hand. It's Budweiser. Not my favorite. Apparently he's the boss of this operation. Ah, Christ its whatshisname, the ex leader guy Geo...

Apparently I said that out loud and as he came and sat beside me while extending a hand and a Budweiser he said, "No the name is Stan!" Brain is waking up. What in the name of matted chicken shit is this guy doing here? With me? This is one baaad hangover! What could I do? I popped the beer! The boss in my head started sending out directions. If this guy is who we think he is then get him to pronounce the word 'nuclear.' Yeah, right. I'm knocked out of my doldrums and I'm supposed to ask this guy to pronounce a word?

He asks if he can fish with my rod for a while. Everyone is dressed casual, could even pass for vacationing fishermen. The aviator glasses were a bit eerie, I mean anyone could pretty much tell who they were. Sure, I says, fish away. It's a lure, I don't use bait, gotta keep the line moving. With that we start up a conversation that ran the gamut of anything and everything that crossed our thoughts. The other dudes just sort of stood in the background every once in a while taking off and polishing their glasses with their shirts. One of them came over and offered me a chicken breast and I accepted. Nothing better with a beer. This guy with my fishing pole was shorter than me and he talked a lot and he smoked cigars. He was no Fidel Castro of course. He was Geo... um...Stan!

We got to know each other a bit and we offed a few beers. He caught a blowfish and a yellowtail which he threw back. We watched a hammerhead swim under the bridge. I asked if he had ever seen TRUE LIES, the Schwarzenegger movie where the nuclear blast took place off the Seven Mile Bridge. Indeed he had. Knew the man well and had cringed when the 'nucular' bomb had gone off. Mr. Brain said that's him, no doubt about it. I agreed and had another beer with the ex-President of the United States of America!

I said that I had heard he had stopped drinking. He had but the daughter's wedding was long and the reception was fabulous and the term was nearly over so... We carried on for about two hours. The Secret Service guys kept bringing beers. He caught more undersized fish but seemed to be having a good time. At points he was hemming and hawing a bit and it appeared he had something uncomfortable to say. I hoped it had nothing to do with the 'Florida Straits. What's your name he asked and I told him and I asked why he called himself Stan. He said he thought he looked more like a Stan than anything else and I said that's the most honest thing I ever heard him say. "Well, I got some more honesty, Jack. I want you to get me into one of those Key West sex clubs without the world finding out about it."

What?

An hour and a half later we're at Betty's Bottled Up Boobies on South Duval. In my position I'm thinking of all the hilarity that's right in front of me yet all the dangers that may ensue. If things went badly couldn't these bodyguards just shoot me and toss me off a bridge? Isn't this guy still married? Am I serving my country? Mr. Brain where are you? Can't ever find him when there's even the slightest scent of sex. Useless.

I tell Stan that we have to lose the Secret Service and the Tahoe for a while. This doesn't go over well with them. We negotiated that two would wait in the restaurant across the street and one would go in just before us as a paying customer. Great, I'm gonna go have a paid sexual adventure in a room next to a room with this other guy that I didn't even vote for whose having sex with who knows who. Hey, aren't most of these girls Russian or Ukraine? Am I leading this guy into an international incident? Isn't this all his idea?

In my room with the brunette we have some nice Indian music and some incense sticks burning. I have a towel over my butt and a naked girl in front of me asking if I want certain extras and telling me there's an ATM in the lobby if I do. I wonder if Stan has enough cash on hand. Of course he does. He's the ex- what the doozy. They've always got cash. Don't they? My new friend Lisa is rubbing my shoulders with some kind of oil and it smells very nice and her hands are individual temptresses sent to me by the ancient Egyptian Pharaohs and, oh, yummy. My my. Dum de dum. Then the yelling in the next room with Stan obviously ticked off about something and one of the aviator guys just stating the facts as he sees them. I reach for my clothes and just then the Key West Vice Squad slams through the front door led by the Chief of Police, a gay and religious man who harbors no illusions as to what is going on in this gilded palace of sin. The two Secret Service crash through the door from across the street and pepper spray the lobby and all the individuals present, including Stan, who, undressed, looks like no one they've ever seen and Mr. Brains says reel. Reel, you idjut. What? Brains never comes to sex pairings! Shots ring out!

What?

Reel, you lunatic. Reel? I reel and reel and reel. There's a seven-foot hammerhead on the end of my line and he's doing the dance of fury. I try to focus and look around for Lisa. There's just a bunch of Cubans on the other side of the bridge and they're jabbering away about blah, blah, blah, shark this, Spanish that. Oh, I've hooked a shark! Right here on the Florida Straits I've got me a seven-foot hammerhead. Goddam!

Imagine that.

YEARS REMOVED FROM THE HAPPY TIME

As a young boy and much later in life I reveled in the adventures attained by exploring the less noticed mangroves.

In these woods which were half water and half tree roots with a smattering of sand and mud I would come across old fishing gear and half sunken boats. There were elements of old clothing, flip-flops, lobster buoys and dock pylons. Sometimes there were the remains of old plane crashes from the Navy planes stationed at Boca Chica. One time I found a fully stocked tackle kit which took me years to deplete. Other times I would run into hobo camps which later turned into camps for the mentally ill, drunk and drug-addled. As troubled people they were a danger to me and I would quickly move on.

One day, as an adult, on the smaller Saddlebacks I chanced into an encampment that was odd because of its comparative neatness when compared to the hobo camps. There was a hut with a thatched roof. There was what appeared to be a front yard and although devoid of grass its hard packed sand and coral was neatly swept. There were many stacks of flotsam and jetsam in neat orderly rows about the hut. There were clothes drying on a line and a small fire that emitted little if any smoke. There was a hammock strung between two palm trees, multiple coolers made of many materials and an old waterlogged picnic table with three or four handguns resting on top.

I reacted with caution to the sidearms. A hobo with a gun was a serious problem indeed! Then out of the twisted roots and rust colored mud appeared an ancient man partially stooped and bearded but whistling in an aura of good feeling. He saw me there on the edge of the camp and stared for a moment. He looked over at the guns on the table and that made me nervous. He looked at me again and said, "Don't vorry, I von't shoot!" Running seemed like a great idea at the moment but I was transfixed.

"You sit, eh?"

What I might do rhymed with sit but somehow, against my better judgment, I approached the table and sat. I looked into the face of a man whose age had apparently been sculpted into it by one of the Italian masters. His hair was the white of a man well into his late seventies or eighties. His teeth were mostly gone but the ones left were well cared for. He offered me a slice of coconut meat and I accepted. We chewed and stared at one another. Where in the world did this ancient mariner come from? Little did I know then of the relevance of my quiet question.

"I haff been vaiting for someone for a very long, long time. Now you are here. Vood you like to talk?"

I saw no disposition in this human being that suggested any intention of harm toward me. Yeah, sure talk away. This'll be one for the book.

For several hours my new friend, Dieter, as he explained, took me on a journey of many years through his life in the mangrove swamps and his existence in the

Lower Keys. There was no recitation as such because I would ask questions and he would answer. Sometimes our remarks would sway over into the weather or what was happening down on Duval Street. We shot the breeze for long minutes on fishing and the best baits for certain kinds of fish. For a few moments we even talked about professional basketball. We became accustomed to one another and friendliness like bougainvillea blossomed between us. This was an exciting old gentleman and I wanted to hear more but the hour was growing late and I begged off till another day. He understood and said that when I returned he would tell me "von helluva goot story!" I told him I couldn't wait and that was the truth. I had discovered my own wreck of the Atocha and I wanted to mine it.

It was several days before I could return and it took an extra day because I couldn't for the life of me remember how I came upon his little settlement. It was quite a walk from where my car was parked out on the old gravel road and I was very worried about its safety. But after a painting job I promised and doing all my grocery shopping for the week I set out for another day with Dieter.

I found him at the same old picnic table once again carving coconut from its shell. He offered me a few bites again and reminded me of the properties involved in eating too much of it. I told him I already knew. He said that today he must relay his story as best he could remember because his time was growing short. What follows is what he relayed. It is not what I expected. At all!

Dieter was born in the Wiemar Republic in Hamburg in 1922. As a young man he enjoyed studying art and in his teen years was able to spend a little time in Paris to perfect his craft and maybe try out the local beer and possibly the girls. His country was going through all kinds of changes and many of them not so good. The Nazis were running everything and these people were not so nice, but as he explained, the economy got much better and everyone's lives began to improve. Up to a point. After the invasion of France he was notified to prepare for military induction. Knowing of the submarine corps he quickly volunteered and was accepted as a Naval Cadet.

In 1942 he was assigned to U-boat 231b and headed off with his shipmates to the east coast of the United States. Dieter did not like sinking ships and taking human life. He did not like Nazis and did not join the party but he was a patriot and did as he was asked. From 1942 until mid-1943 the U-boat commanders in the Atlantic described their experiences as the "Happy Time." Millions of tons of allied shipping were sunk versus the loss of very few U-boats. The allies were certainly not winning the war!

At the end of August 1942 his ship was ordered into the Caribbean and then into the Gulf of Mexico. U231b sank five freighters, two oilers, a patrol craft and several Coast Guard Auxiliary craft. Most of these ships were sunk with the submarine's deck gun while on the surface at night. Dieter had seen much mayhem and madness and watched as men on the opposing ships burned to death or drowned while swallowing crude oil. The Happy Time was not happy for him. The few times that mail had gone out he told his family of his travails. The last time he sent mail he received mail. His mother, father, and two sisters had been incinerated in a nighttime British bombing raid. The Third Reich was very sorry!

Two weeks later while surfaced on an ill-advised daytime sortie with a German Milch Cow a squadron of Navy Helldivers and a bevy of Grumman Wildcats attacked the nursing sub and it was holed substantially. The Milch Cow was blown all to hell with no survivors. The captain ordered U231b submerged despite its injuries. Because of its mortal injuries, it could submerge no lower than 20 feet. Then it drifted below the surface for three days subjected to constant bombardment and aerial depth-charging. On the evening of the third day the captain ordered abandon ship and the crew dispersed in seven rubber boats. Six boats were captured the next day by a cutter out of Key West. The seventh drifted for about a week until it beached on a mangrove somewhere north of Big Pine Key. There were injured and dead aboard. Six got ashore.

After several days it was apparent that a mangrove would not prolong anyone's life, so they set off for a dryer spot. The dryer spot turned out to be just a few yards from where I had met Dieter. In the next several days all of the enlisted crewman set off for friendlier grounds only to be captured on the Overseas Highway by the Military Police. Dieter's friend, Manny, the navigator, survived with him until he died in 1953 of malaria.

Dieter and Manny had many supplies on their lifeboat. There were guns, fishing tackle, clothing and fresh water for a while. There were matches, canned food, flashlights, batteries, knives and first aid kits. When their friends never returned they kept low and only lit fires very late at night. They survived on fish, coconut and made raids into the vegetable gardens of the few locals that lived in the backcountry of Saddleback Key.

They knew when the war had ended and chose to stay. Eventually they would come out of the mangroves to mingle with the community and took odd jobs and sometimes stole clothing from backyards. Manny wanted to go home but Dieter was comfortable in this world. They both worried about being imprisoned. The years passed as did Manny but Dieter kept with his course. Over time he held several jobs in the Keys and no one ever questioned his accent. After he turned sixty he kept more and more to himself and seldom ventured out unless he needed medical supplies from a drug store. Then loneliness became a way of life. He was aware, from newspaper accounts, of the many Japanese who had holed up after the war. He didn't understand it. While they held a devotion to the emperor he held none to Adolf Hitler. He was orphaned and so began a regimented life that suited him and went into the world only when the need was intense.

"Goot story, ya?"

I told him it was an excellent story and that I had my doubts. But first I needed to go home and blend all this information together in my mind. He understood and so I took my leave promising to see him the following week. I drove home in a delirium knowing that I had met the world's hugest lunatic or one of creation's greatest survivors. I tried to sleep but kept questioning my sanity. I tried to keep sane then slept.

I returned four days later. There was no smoldering to the campfire. The raccoons had been through the place. The guns and Dieter were spread out on the picnic table. He was quite dead and had been for some days. Birds and insects had already been at him. I stared at my new friend for a very long time and found myself crying for the poor man. I took it upon myself to bury him and took on the chore knowing that the coral was going to be a tough dig. Upon completion I erected a cross and carved in the words, "Dieter, a good man." In his little neatly kept shack I found a note. It said, "Tell them I was never a Nazi, never!"

I found some lighter fluid, a little gasoline and some cooking oil. I spread it over the shack, picnic table and stacks of flotsam and lit it aflame. I stood at attention and saluted the good sailor. I went home and while staring out the window I uncorked a fresh bottle of tequila and took a healthy shot. I'm pretty sure I can face anything. Now.

THINGS GET SILLIER ON THE BRIDGE

Out of the corner of my eye I see him approaching on his bicycle. It appears that he's carrying another bike. It's a sure sign of theft.

As per usual I'm fishing, catching nothing, caught up in my tropical reveries and looking for absolutely no companionship. I got beer in my cooler, some smokes and 58 years of memories to contemplate upon. Hope this guy doesn't stop. Where can you steal a bike out here in the middle of nowhere? It's my lucky day because he stops and asks that age-old question that never ceases to irritate: "Catch anything?"

Then he proceeds to ask if I want to buy a unicycle, the one-wheeled contraption that I had assumed was a stolen bike. Um, I'm fishing. I'm daydreaming. And some nut wants to know if I want to buy a unicycle out here on my religious pedestal, my philosophical bastion, in the middle of my thoughts where no other human is welcome? What's worse is he's a talker. The kind of people who made me take an oath to stay out of bars for fear of discussing idiocy. Trapped. I'm trapped in the wide-open spaces right in front of the Florida Straits with nothing on the horizon to hinder my vision but sky and blue-green water because someone wants to sell me a UNICYCLE?

He saw the plates on my car and asks where I'm from in Connecticut. I tell him and he says he never heard of it. I tell myself that's why I lived there. He says he's from Worcester and I begin to notice certain eye movements and body tics. It's a nut who wants to sell me a unicycle. Just great. Stupidly I tell him I went to Clark University. What did you study? Psychology (a lie). Do you have your own practice? he asks after making an assumption. No (the truth). Worked in hospitals (the truth). What kind of people did you work with? I wanted to say people like you. People who approach a stranger on a bridge and ask if they want to buy a unicycle.

For the next half hour I get a complete rundown of his life in Worcester, all the rock stars he's met, and by the way did you know Eric Clapton always has an extra hotel room to set up his personal pool table in? You don't say. Pretty soon all I hear is a droning monologue concerning who knows what while I continue casting and reeling in. I wonder what Sandie is doing up in Portsmouth and Eugene over in Newport. Is there going to be that real good peeled shrimp at Alonzo's tonight? "...And then me and Fleetwood Mac partied down at the Irish bar in the north end till dawn. Boy that dude was blasted!" Oh yeah, Fleetwood Mac is a single man? The guy's eyes rolled up in his head and I was looking at white where they used to be.

I don't know if he caught the hint or just used up the last piece of his cognizant abilities because he left and there I was standing alone, by myself, not surrounded by anyone else. Barracuda took the line and ran with it. I wasn't interested in pulling him in because of the hook removal versus sharp teeth debacle that was bound to ensue but, hey, it was a fish and I was alone, and, who knows, maybe a past sexcapade will jump into my brain now that no one else is here. If you can't have sex at least you can remember it!

I was slowly packing up the fishing gear in my car but not in any way wanting to depart. I headed over to one of the picnic tables with the open roof thingamabob and sat and just stared out to sea with an ice-cold buddy to keep me company. The fighter jets were doing their thing and were fun to watch and, besides, I like jet noise. I finished up the coldie and walked over to my car where a Monroe County deputy sheriff had just pulled up. She introduced herself as Dottie and we shot the breeze for a while. She said I shouldn't park in front of the closed gate in case there ever was an emergency. I told her I couldn't foresee any emergency ever occurring here.

Well, apparently while I was up bluegrassing this past summer some guy had decided to hang himself from the picnic roof thingamabob. A tourist intent on stopping on the bridge and asking someone how the fishing was going had seen him and called the sheriff. The paramedics had to get a car towed just so they could remove the body. That tow last summer cost 400 smackers. The county commission got together since then and cut down on predatory towing practices and outrageous pricing. The towing company didn't collect on the car. It belonged to the dead man. The deputy and I shot the shit for a while. I kinda thought she was flirting with me and that didn't suck.

"By the way," she asked before departing, "did you see a guy trying to hock a unicycle?"

ONE STREET OFF OF WHITEHEAD

One street off of Whitehead I'm kibitzing on the second-floor balcony of my friend's apartment. I'm a few days removed from a feline attack that swelled my arm to such an extent that I called the paramedics. Things got better for the arm and I'm sure the attack was one of mistaken identity.

This Sunday morning guests at the hotel across the street started honking their horn while backing out of their parking spot. Church was in service at the local Sister's of the Holy Rollers in Bahama Village. There was some pretty good Christmas music coming from the Sisters and the honking wasn't fitting in. This is a very basic tourist being a very basic jerk. I've got the Sopranos on TV and I'm tempted to yell off the balcony something in Italianese that represents 'fungool' in a very basic way.

Although it is low tourist season there's plenty of them around. But their low numbers means that a long walk will be comfortable and somewhat entertaining. The Banyan Tree, a real tree, on the southern part of Whitehead holds my interest for some time. Someone planted this here a long long time ago. Banyans, like palms, aren't native to the keys. This gigantic tree has grown long thick tassels that have ventured downward and replanted themselves in the ground. It has appeared to have created its own supports to steady it in old age.

Walking onto Mallory Square it is soon obvious that there are no crowds whatsoever on this day at noon. It's only a partial pleasure as there are two huge cruise ships tied to the docks. They are high rises like from New York City and block out the sun. Thankfully one is leaving and the other is obligated to before the time of sunset. And then the cat guy will be out and doing his tricks with his trained cats. Where do you get patience to train housecats?

Walking along I come across a massive tattooed fat guy in Bermuda shorts walking his pig. Nice jeweled leash and a diamond collar. I'm in Weirdville and these things just happen. The pig grunts in what seems to be disapproval of my nice clean and neat demeanor. I've got no reason to insult a pig so I move on. For an hour or so I walk the dock areas. There's no need to traipse along Duval or Greene Street with everyone wanting to sit on the stool Hemingway sat on. You can smell the urinal cakes on the sidewalk out front of Captain Tony's. Did enough time at the Village Pub in New Haven during college. Really don't feel like quaffing a beer with that aromatic yet pungent odor permeating my thought processes. I want to give the guitar player's name to one of the Soprano captains and maybe a kiss on both cheeks.

I end up back at my friend's apartment on the second-floor balcony. The cat that had mistaken me as an aggressive Samurai is sitting on an outside chair and purring for forgiveness. Can I do anything else? We kick back and wait for the Patriot's game that comes on at four. The southeasterlies are blowing as they have done for the past two weeks. I'm going to stare off the balcony for several hours and commiserate with old spirits that haven't been around for some time. We have some talking to do.

MORE ASPHALT ON WHITEHEAD

Sometimes you wonder what made you do the things you did. Why did you pack up everything and move yourself down to the islands and put every little important thing on the back burner? Why did you ball up newspaper and put a match to it to start an even larger fire? You can sit and contemplate and even think you've figured it all out but you haven't although you've convinced yourself otherwise. You tell yourself its a guy thing and you content yourself with your answer and spend endless hours fishing and hanging out at a bridge in the middle of nowhere thinking that you're mulling over life's never-ceasing problems.

Sometimes you wonder things like this and all of a sudden the big fat guy in Bermuda shorts with a leash connected to a pig walks back into your life. It may be a footnote to a thesis but there it is; 450 pounds of bacon dragging an equally fat poorly dressed guy through the streets of Key West. Do you have the right, therefore, to contemplate the universe, your navel or the end days of Karma?

What you do is forget everything that is dragging you down and get out on the street and enjoy your environment. This won't be the only pig you meet. Your maker will judge you on how you handle your pork. So off

43

it is to the Parrot and some human companionship and the forgetting of the delicacies that you have been privileged to enjoy over the last few years.

So for several hours I drank beer with some fat guy in Bermuda shorts who had a pig on a leash festooned with a lot of jewelry. The pig was a sow and still quite young and I'd have to say I've had worse dates. The beer was cold, the conversation was fair and I didn't worry about even one little thing this way or the other. When things are absurd just go with it. I've got tons of friends who married for the very same reason.

WHITEHEAD, PART III

Riding around on the old girl's Conch bike I drift into the traffic pattern.

The jets are landing at the airport at about five per hour, all the Conch Trains are full, the tourist busses likewise and there's no purpose to try and get a picture at the Southernmost Spot. As if I'd want to. But the easterlies are still blowing, the sun flits in and out of clouds, and I permeate myself into the mysticism of this place. How soon before I run into some oddness heretofore not made obvious?

Well, as a matter of fact, as I watch from the sidewalk in front of the lighthouse a car pulls up into their parking lot and parks in the handicapped spot. Five people emerge, and although not young, not aged or decrepit either. The reason to park here is to purchase a ticket so that you can climb the lighthouse via a spiral staircase about 250 straight up. One would think the only reason for a handicapped spot might be for a handicapped person. Not if you're from New Jersey.

A friend from Philadelphia recently told me he caught a non-handicapped person parking in one of those spots. As he related, "He'll never do THAT again!" Just can't repair some people. The bike pedals itself on up United Street and the Grand Poincianas shade my progress.

There was a trailer park for navy families on United Street in 1961. I lived there and once climbed a Grand

Poinciana but slipped and scraped my chest on a nail that some previous kid had hammered into the tree knowing some day there would be a victim. Still have that scar. The trailer park is still there and I pass it on my ancient Conchocycle on my way to who knows where. The contraption proceeds at my direction onto Watson and then Truman Avenue. As I stop a motorcycle with a sidecar passes. In the sidecar a pig is seated with wraparound sunglasses and a Red Baron scarf. So long guys.

On Truman I pass the Gay Lesbian Center. Out front is an old Conch redneck dressed in dirty unkempt clothes holding a sign that says all fags are going to hell. Next to him a neatly dressed middle aged gay fellow holding a sign with an arrow on it pointing to the Conch. The sign reads: "Village Idiot"! All you can do is laugh out loud. I shake the hand of the neatly dressed guy so that the Conch knows where I'm coming from. To incorrectly paraphrase the Louis Armstrong song: "What a weirdass wonderful world!"

Over near the docks on Caroline the sun shines in joyous epiphanies. It's sitting on the stone wall time just for the pleasure of observing. Oddly nothing odd happens. After a half hour of this it's get to the store, stock up on some beer and ice and load the baskets on the Conchocycle. Back up on the balcony with a cold one and some good reggae music playing on the radio.

Catty cornered to the balcony rises the lighthouse. In the space between lies the space where my friend, Henry the chicken, met his end. The lighthouse looks good there. It's certainly got a majesty to it and it reigns over its dominions. Kinda looks like a yard ornament from this angle. Like to put some cheap paper propellers on it and make it into a giant whirlygig. From the bottom emerges five folks not in the least gasping for air. They go over to the handicapped parking spot and get into their Lincoln MX with power steering, power brakes, power windows and special privileges.

MOTHER S ETERNAL SKY

One afternoon in very early July I get to put myself and my camper onto a field on a large mountain with vistas that were given to me by my maker. While the sun is still up I commit myself to my campsite but I often just stand and stare at this gift that has been bestowed upon me. Views like this were never ever considered to be the best thought put into a postcard. I'm near the top of the Catskills. The sun etches my shadow as if in a personal favor. The warmth is like a mother's pat on the back.

Through the day I continue my many endeavors but I don't stress. With this weather and this climate I'm brought together with nature and one-li-ness. To be one and have no requirements is a sweetness that isn't conferred upon a person very often. The sun hangs like an adjusted light on a studio desk. The shadows get longer but the light and the warmth hang around as old friends and quietly assist me.

Much later its 10:15 pm and I'm watching the Milky Way stretch its way across my vision. An old friend it reminds me that it remembers who I am and hopes I'm happy that I've been pulled away from the reaches of city lights. Even in the country Providence casts a lighted pall on my existence some twenty miles away. But I'm not anywhere near Providence. I'm on top of a mountain 200 miles away and I have no sound but for the wind and no visuals but for the Milky Way. A woman would be nice but this is sublime. At some point I fall asleep outside and drift into eternity until near light I'm aroused on the grass by the heaviness of the dew. I look up and see the Milky Way is gone. There is an orange circle coming up out of the cooler of the far east. Coffee comes to my mind and I make preparations. Birds begin a chorus and I tell them I don't know the words.

At some indeterminate point another person shows up. It is a person same as me. Needs no thoughts on directions or advice. She just begins doing what she thinks is best for a large crowd and doesn't need input. She gets her tent up and some friends' follow. We have hours of beautiful sky and talking about our relatives. We have 12 hours before the first family member. The Milky Way comes back and we stretch our necks and comment on the Big Dipper and Pleiades. A family of deer slowly graze in the dusk just a few yards away. At some points quiet and other points noisy we revel in ourselves and our relationships and sometimes what we mean to each other.

In the morning there is not just the first camper and guitar player but thoughts on the Health Department who threatens to show up. There's thoughts on the water truck, the portolets and all that stuff that goes with this enterprise. This isn't a large enterprise but it's a fun thing that has responsibilities. The hill is resplendent with responsible people. We get together and agree: "Responsible, yeah, right!"

The days move along and the sun shines and sings its summer song. Down the hill pretty soon now. It's another chapter. And God gave this to me. Gave it to us.

FREEDOM

Sadness and fate sometimes coincide in the Maker's larger plan. So it was on a January morning in 1994 in a small boat out of Cuba on a run to freedom.

Mariel and Jose Arrida, their daughter Rose and friend Paco set off in a ten-foot boat with a small and ancient Evinrude motor with ten gallons of gas, a mast with a cotton sail, and dreams of redemption in a country called the United States. The winds were light, the seas were fairly calm and they set off from a small town ten miles east of Havana.

The sun shone with a weak warmth and everyone's thoughts were positive and expectant toward a new life as soon as they set foot on American soil. Even when the breeze picked up and the cloudless sky became overcast there was no need for worry. Mariel breast-fed Rose while Paco and Jose talked of their soon-to be-newly-found wealth. It was a cheerful trip from the start. The Evinrude droned for about an hour until the Cuban coast disappeared in the haze. It was then they set up the small cotton sail and shut the engine down. They had about seven gallons left and they were determined to use it only in case of emergency. The swells were only about four feet and there was no reason for fear.

Mariel gave the baby over to Jose and took her turn on the old wooden tiller. They were aiming for Marathon or Key Largo depending on the wind, tides and luck that every small-time mariner needed. Soon Paco and Mariel were talking about the wonderful Cuban cornbread and smoked fish and rice that they had many times enjoyed. There was only some yellow rice and water on the boat for supplies and they were determined to eat and drink sparingly. The three had one suitcase apiece, the clothes on their backs and shoes on their feet. Mariel and Paco spoke and dreamed of past meals and the day settled into dusk while the baby and Jose slept.

After dark all four were in or near a state of sleep and the boat drifted and sometimes sailed wherever it pleased. The boat rocked a lullaby and dreams of freedom were frequent and real.

At dawn Jose awoke and saw the last of the sun and noticed it was in the wrong place. He also saw that the chop had picked up and the swell had increased. He awoke his wife and gave her the baby. The boat was taking on water and Jose saw that one of the things he had forgotten was something to bail with. Fear opened a little door in the back of his mind and he sought solutions to his present and future predicaments. But freedom was his ambition and his life's goal and he would not give in to nature or any of its problems. He sought only solutions in his mind and quietly he plotted the future.

In an hour the future plotted itself as the chop and swell increased to a degree that did not include a small boat with four people within. Then came the wind! It came in gusts and gales and splashes of salt water that immersed everyone in a cold bone-soaking misery. Paco held onto the gunwales and Mariel held onto her baby.

For hour upon hour they were tossed about as toys from young children. The sun completely disappeared and daylight darkness encompassed the whole of their surroundings. Jose had Paco and himself take off their shirts to soak up the water from the bottom of the boat in a continuous dunking and wringing of cloth. The baby cried and Mariel fretted as she prayed to the Good Mother for salvation.

When Jose and Mariel had married the whole town had gathered to celebrate. They had privileges as Mariel's uncle was a party member and provided for them a slaughtered pig and imported beer for the wedding. Jose had provided for his small family by rolling tobacco in the famous cigar trade and this was a job that earned him enough to ask her hand in marriage. They had an adequate home albeit the roof was one of thatch. They had no car but her uncle had previously provided them with a donkey for household and gardening chores. Mariel loved her tomato garden and sold at the market once every Saturday. But the money was poor, the thatch roof leaked and Jose had a cousin in Miami. After the wedding feast they made their first inroads into thoughts that they might escape. It was nice to have an uncle who was well connected but this was no way to live. They would have to leave their families and create a life for their newly born daughter. With a hundred dollars saved from wedding gifts they bought a small boat and obtained a small amount of fuel. Paco, another cousin, learned of the plan and begged to go. Jose felt good about having another man and a hand around to help with the many problems ahead. The day arrived. They left. They told no one. They just left.

The wind now was beyond a gale and the boat was not built for such a rough encounter with nature. Huge waves were spilling into the boat and no amount of soaking shirts and wringing them out was going to help. The wind was a fearsome thing and Mariel held onto her child. Hour after hour they were tossed from one wave to another; from one swell to the next. The cotton sail existed no more, the water in the bottom of the boat increased in depth. And still the storm increased! Water dwarfed the boat from mountainous heights and the wind blew salt into the eyes of the pilgrims. Then, God turned his back.

At some point Paco thought he saw land and screamed to his friends that salvation was at hand. But they didn't hear as at that moment the boat overturned and all were thrown into the tumult! Mariel and her baby were separated from the men immediately and began to drift with the roaring seas. Jose dove after her and his beloved child just as the small mast that held the pitiful sail collapsed into the ocean and onto his head. Jose softly and quietly dipped below the surface as his family drifted away. Paco clung to the overturned boat and cried for his mother, his creator or any deity that might do favor unto him. He was unheard. His world turned in various degrees from white to gray to black. The sea continued its quest to cleanse itself of unwelcome guests and roared in tempest!

Paco awoke in the cabin of a motorized vehicle moving at a very high rate of speed. He was in a boat called a "go fast" and is used only for the smuggling of people or drugs. In his case the boat was carrying nearly half a ton of cocaine from the coast of Mexico to some non-specified port or islet in the Florida Keys. He knew none of this. As he appeared on deck he met the captain, his savior, at about the same time as a US Coast Guard Cutter intercepted the boat. The boat added some incredible speed but the Coast Guard fired a few shells from their three-inch fifties into the water in front of their bow. The crew began tossing the drugs overboard. There was land no less than a mile to the port side. It was America and in only ten minutes, if he could land his feet, he would be a free man. His good friends Jose and Mariel and their child wouldn't be with him but he would be a free man. An American!

The boat was stopped. Everyone was arrested including Paco, who not knowing English could not explain his predicament or his recent trials or the loss of his close friends. He got to see Miami. He got to set his feet on American soil and feel the freedom he had so long yearned. It was a terrible trip and the sacrifice was immense and it was all more than Paco's mind could endure.

When after the trial Paco could understand what had happened to him he had been sentenced to ten years in federal prison for drug running. Year after year he cursed his fate but held out that he was at least finally an American. Then the day came when he was put on the same Coast Guard Cutter and returned to Havana. There he received a sentence handed down by the Revolutionary Court for being an anti-revolutionary and spent two more years in prison, although by his own reasoning the food was better. He now rolls cigar leaves in the same factory as his old friend Jose. Somewhere along the line he came into the custody of a female feline who became his best friend. He called her Rose.

Twelve years earlier on a small sand spit just below a tangled mass of mangroves on the Lower Saddlebunches a bundle of human forms washed up with the tide. There appeared to be no life and death hovered on the wind in its expectancy. Yet breath emanated from each soul and joined with the living of each and every specie pumping blood through its veins. Although living death was nigh and thereabouts a savior was in desperate need. There was little hope and these three appeared to use the last of luck left in their accounts. Out of the mangroves appeared a fourth shipwrecked survivor. As the clouds dispersed and the sun shone through Dieter knelt by the sides of each family member and began to minister unto them.

CATCH ANYTHING?

I just want to fish and be left alone.

Some days that isn't about to happen. Everybody wants to stop on the bridge and ask if I've caught anything. They ask despite the fact I don't have a fish bucket and there are no half dead fish lying around. "No, its a slow day," I say. "Maybe tomorrow."

The best thing to do is go home. And I do and sit down in the mancave surrounded by green hanging plants that I have recently collected and pop open a beer and light up a smoke. Nice day, warm, no attacking armies. The parachutists fall through the sky across the canal and I can hear the whoosh when the fabric expands in the air. There's no fish today but there's no worries so I settle my eyes on a cloud formation and drift into some other time and remember things that were meant to be remembered. The sun gently slides onto its living room sofa and its aura touches the horizon on the Gulf. And a few mosquitos start biting my legs.

Fairly soon there's a keg party of my blood going and every skeeter in the county feels obliged to stop by. First the retirees show up in their obnoxious old folks summer attire and blue hair. They take their bites and pretty soon you hear (slap) and then (slap on the ankle) and then (slap on the forehead) and then some teenagers show up and they're listening to rap music and (slap on the other ankle) and acting like asswipes. Shortly thereafter a middle-aged skeeter flies by with a six-pack of beer with three beers missing and I'm thinking (slap) that he's seen too many episodes of WKRP in Cincinnati. One skeeter sets up a tiny table on my knee and whips out a deck of cards. He's yapping all the while talking about Catholics this and Cubans that and the universe is ever expanding...and stuff.

Shortly the biker skeeters show up and they're all flexing their muscles and showing their tattoos and daring other dudes to fight. A gaggle of single skeeter girls show up in mini skirts and halter tops and finally a bunch of bugs with guitars and bongos and they start playing old rock songs and smoking (slap) pot. I'm hanging in there. After all, I'm the host.

It's totally dark now and a slight breeze alights. The lightweight skeeters start passing out or flying home but I've still got the bikers and (slap) the rappers. I put on some bug rub. Eventually the party thins out but I can hear straight pipes receding loudly in the distance. The rappers finally leave after displaying their boxer shorts five inches above the waistline of their pants. Mosquitos sure have changed since I was a boy. (slap).

The next day I went to the bridge and began fishing. It was a beautiful day with tons of sun and only a slight breeze. My mind was tens of thousands of miles away. I was winning the lottery, I was having sex with one of the girls from 'Friends', I was solitary and flatulent. And then a mosquito with a baby grand flew up to my ear and began playing 'Winter' by George Winston. He had been to the party the night before and knew of my preference to this type of music. He gave me 50 minutes of a wonderful interlude between the trials of life and being.

As he winded up his solo work a rented red convertible Mustang pulled up with a gray-haired, pony-tailed though balding man smiling through his gold caps. He looked over at his passenger, an equally balding middle-aged woman chain-smoking Marlboros and gave her a smile. Almost in unison they asked, "catch anything?" My piano-playing friend whipped out his cell phone and within minutes the teenagers, the bikers and the retirees had accumulated out of what seemed nowhere and proceeded to acclimate to the persons entombed in the insides of this Florida pony car. Luckily (slap) I got home before the frenzy.

No, I didn't catch anything.

WALKING A DAVID CROSBY SONG

Got mail, gas, shopped and said, what the hell, let's go to Bahia Honda. It was only five miles from the store.

The closely shaved flora rises up after the entrance and suddenly envelopes you for several hundred feet. All green and unimposing. My nose found the favorite beach spot. The keys turned themselves off and the car kicked me out. I tossed the shirt, patted the beer belly and walked onto a sunshiny stretch of white sand. Now what?

I got on a beach once in Sarasota somewhere around Siesta Key and put my feet into 85-degree water with a very warm breeze blowing. The coast to the north and south stretched out beyond vision and every half a mile or so you could see little clumps of people and that looked a little interesting so I sauntered on over that half a mile and found a mom and two little kids. Damn! There's another clump about another half mile up the beach. Looks interesting too! A gorgeous sky and sun massaged every muscle on my body and the walk was doing me good.

Fairly obviously I kept deceiving myself with mirages on the shore at a distance from my being. You know, my car's five miles down the beach. Then I'm humming the old song about, "Lookin' in your mirror and seein' a police car...". Shoulda thought up a different song. It was a long walk.

Back in the Bahia Honda present I hit the beach and plant my feet in the sand very deeply. Offer my face to the sun. Great to be alive some days. A young couple comes up behind me and I can hear the girl saying that maybe they should head off down the beach where all those people are. If there had been a motion picture camera trained on me I would have turned around and winked. Wonder what the hell Flo is doin'? C'mon feet, don't fail me now.

Driving down to Weirdtown the radio belts out a Jimmy Buffett song about jumping on the equator and not knowing if he's up or if he's down. I try to make it that today the mind is not too engaged. Should be easy. Second verse, same as the first! I got food, beer and cigs and there's Flo's driveway. May as well bring in the computer to see if a stray thought might fly by that's usable.

We shoot the shit in that easy familiar way and achieve cocktailness. Joss, the cat, creeps up from underneath a parked car downstairs to see his old buddy whose arm he once scratched severely enough to have him call an ambulance. Now that I know that Joss is the alpha male here we have come to an understanding. As long as I keep my nose out of his business concerning other growling cats and just go play on my little computer and be the two-legged idiot everything will be OK. He said it, I obeyed and I'm playing on my little computer.

Joss brought home a young baby bird one day recently and a growling cat came with him. There was a whole fiasco again with the same two cats but no human got hurt. The bird seems to have had just enough feathers and strength to jump off the balcony and fly a distance away. Birds to cats down here are slices of Key Lime Pie.

On mindless days like these I print tripe and Flo sits across from me typing on her computer dissertations about Turkish families who practice some sort of incest and there's a word for that but its so weird I decided to not even write it down. Three syllables are about my limit for today. Taking a Walk with a David Crosby song will probably come back some time soon. Maybe even tonight.

THE LIGHT AND THE DARK

My mother and stepfather were not meant for each other. They had cheating hearts. Maybe all of us do but if children are involved there surely must be a better agenda.

My stepfather was a cruel, physically manipulating man that would throw a knife at a child and beat the blood out of a woman until she was so lost in her own mind that she had to be consigned to a mental ward in a Naval Hospital. At the age of eight I knew and saw all these things and more. I took my relief in the Huck Finn existence that was afforded me when we were all transferred, Navy style, to a magical place called Key West.

In 1960 I had finished the second grade. I had spent the previous two years in Wickford, Rhode Island, some 1500 miles from my birthplace of Sarasota, Florida. I had seen blizzards. I had seen Hurricane Donna and watched as the Ford Falcon we owned, tied down with chains, fight against the wind from being flipped into eternity. It was certainly exciting. One day we found that we were to be moved by the government as a whole family to the southern environs. Back from where I was born.

But I had never been to Key West. What kind of place was this? I heard the adults talking and heard a lot about island paradise and fishing and warm weather and so forth. Better than snow! Isn't a child's life all about wonderment?

We drove out of Rhode Island and down the eastern seaboard on old route 1. In those days the Eisenhower Interstate System was in its infancy. It may have taken two whole days just to get to Virginia! There were lots of motel stops along the way. There were four children and two adults in a Ford Falcon. This wasn't a large vehicle. It had the same chassis as the Model T. I had brothers yelling and screaming and a sister getting sick on scrambled eggs and cheese and puking all over the duffel bags that held our clothes. There was no comfortable. Comfortable was for some rich people driving in Cadillacs and Lincolns!

When we got to Columbia, South Carolina, a little off our track, the old man broke down and bought a used Oldsmobile 88. We stayed with his parents for a few nights. I remember raking up some leaves and trash in his yard for ten centavos. I thought ten centavos was ten dimes. After working an hour I got ten cents. Even at my age at the time I knew a rip off when I saw one. Suddenly we were back on the road. I was too young to know about Jack Kerouac at the time but later I came to realize what he spoke of when transpiring his adventures while traveling. There really is nothing like the road. The destination isn't the end of the means. The growth of your inner self while experiencing what you see during your travels is the ideal. I was traveling. I was experiencing.

Somewhere in mid-Florida on some back two-lane road north of Palatka we came upon an aviary and we stopped. My stepfather had a Super 8 camera and my mother took film of him as he experimented with tethering and fighting hawks and eagles and falcons. It was terrifying to me but the old man loved it. He had some kind of craziness in his eyes that I would come to know later. These birds were huge and dazzling and thrilling and my stepfather seemed to have mastered them. I was in total awe of a future tyrant and controlling individual who would leave an everlasting mark!

After going through the Everglades and seeing Seminole encampments and wondering about their vivid-colored sweaters (it was winter) we came out on the first bridge of forty-two that would lead us to Key West. The roads were narrow and the bridges even much more so. I was so scared when we went over the old Bahia Honda Bridge. The only similar bridge I knew of at the time, and still to this time, was the old Jamestown Bridge connecting the mainland in Rhode Island to Jamestown (in those days you took a ferry to get to Newport). Bahia Honda was a shocker to me. I hid down on the floorboards so I wouldn't have to see the Gulf on one side, and the Caribbean on the other so far below. I don't remember from then if the Seven Mile Bridge came before or after (I do now) but the enormity of fear that welled up from inside was so much more than my young heart could take. It was a tiny two-lane highway that stretched all those miles! My God we're gonna drive off into the ocean and never be seen again!

When I recovered my senses we were on Big Pine Key and I saw these German Shepherds that seemed out of place to my small mind. Why were there so many? Who would let so many dogs travel along together without any authority to corral and seduce them? They were Key Deer. About two and a half feet high. They were tame and gentle and beautiful and just what a young kid needed after journeying across half the country and 90 miles out to sea.

Overcoming emotional obstacles and traveling so far and seeing such gorgeous creatures was a turning point for my trip. We stopped at a bar where the parents had a few beers and talked to the bartender about what lay ahead. They bought me some pork rinds and a coke and I watched as the colored lights in the Falstaff sign went up and then down in its magical never-ending traverse.

We traveled over Sugarloaf Key, then Boca Chica and then onto Stock Island. I was amazed at all the water that surrounded me. I saw all those families and individuals fishing off the bridges whether for enjoyment or to obtain an evening meal I didn't know. Then I saw the sign that said, "Key West, a bird sanctuary". At that young age, ignorant in all my totality, I knew that all I needed was a Becky Thatcher! It was 1960. The world, and myself, were going to go through some manifestly large and horrible changes.

- – – -

The wind is a roiling gale outside! The chill and dampness permeates my soul although I refuse to turn on the furnace when a couple of heavy shirts should suffice. The cold that is coming only reminds me of the frost that endures deep inside. I crave warmth like any other whether in the environmental sense or the heat of compassionate companionship.

So I reconcile my thoughts to warmer climates in my youth where a fishing pole was my companion and the sun was my friend. If it were summer vacation I'd get out of bed, eat breakfast, and just dissipate from the rest of the family until dark. The consequences of which would put a switch on my backside. It was something one got used to.

In Key West a Naval family got used to the idea that they would live in a trailer in a trailer park until appropriate housing opened up. Until it did I freelanced. I went out into the Pirate Kingdom!

But mostly I went fishing. The old man bought a lot of used fishing rods right off the bat. When he was nice he took me fishing and I would enjoy a sunny day on a bridge or some mangrove swamp fishing for red snapper or grouper. When left to myself I would steal a couple of quarters from the change jar and run off and buy shrimp because that was always the best bait. Fish would bite chopped squid but it was like the choice between pizza and collard greens. The fish and I came to an understanding. I would never insult them with chopped squid or sliced minnows. As my reward I would almost always catch three or four regular snapper and a small grouper or two. I'd take them home and my mother would clean them, flour them up and cook them in grease on a skillet with hush puppies and French fries. What I caught was the family meal at least twice a week.

There were other things going on though. I was enamored with Naval aircraft. In those days there were still fighter planes being used that saw action in World War II. They flew out of the Naval Air Station on Boca Chica, the next island over. There were also Phantom jet fighters, P2V Submarine Chasers, Crusader fighter-bombers and more. In those days the Navy still used the huge seaplanes leftover from the previous wars. It was great fun watching them take off and land in the harbor between the two islands. Over the next two decades they were relegated to Coast Guard duty and finally disappeared altogether in lieu of helicopters. I got to go inside some of these great aircraft and for days after I would daydream about what a great war hero I could become if only I could pilot one of them. I was nine. Dreams came and went. I wasn't politically aware but I did know that something was beginning to happen militarily. You couldn't help but notice. But I was a kid being a kid. The adults would take care of everything, I thought.

The big hobby in those days was building plastic fighter planes, bombers, destroyers, PT boats and battleships. Whenever we got 75 cents we would go to the Western Auto and shop for a new model plane. I loved the Japanese Zero, the Hellcat, the Wildcat and numerous other weapons of the skies. I was a baby boom kid. My real father served in the Army Air Corps in France and Belgium during World War II. I was taught from day one that the Japs were our mortal enemies and would not refrain from cutting our young hearts out! This was how you were taught in my youth. If you didn't accept it you were out of the loop. When my friends and I made battleships out of used two by fours and other scrap wood and set them on the ocean and threw rocks at them we were always the shore battery or the American fleet coming to the rescue! We were preteen militarists. Tojo would have been proud to have us.

Sometimes, at school, we would go on a field trip. One time we rode on the Conch Train and saw all the sights that a tourist would see. As we already lived there and knew the sights it was quite redundant. But who doesn't like a day out of school? Another time we went to the John J. Audubon House. Audubon was the premier painter of birds on the planet during his day. His house was beautiful and majestic. His paintings were like photographs to me. It was beyond my comprehension that a person could put oil to canvas and create such beauty. We also visited the Hemingway House. I didn't understand why we went there. I didn't know who he was or what he did. All I knew was that there sure were a lot of cats hanging about acting like they owned the joint. We didn't go in. The great man was still alive. Many years later I discovered his literature, became enamored with it, and tried to emulate. Ernest is not emulatable.

Horribly I had a BB gun and started to use it. In the summer exotic birds of all colors and sizes would migrate to Key West to escape the South American winters. They were so colorful and pretty and unfortunately sitting ducks to a kid with a BB gun after they had tired themselves out after flying two thousand miles. I would sit in a mangrove swamp and just wait for one to show up and plain and simply plug him. Shortly I began to see that this was not sport. They were too tired to fly away when I approached and simply looked at me with questioning eyes. I've had questioning eyes from women, children and even dogs. They all had their reasons for looking at me in that strange investigative way. What was I up to? I can't say in any instance. I did what I thought I was supposed to do. I played with children. I threw sticks for dogs. I flirted with women and I shot exotic birds with a tiny little gun. For the rest of my life I kindly declined when asked to go hunting.

When I was a kid in Key West, Hollywood came to town and made the movie "PT 109". This was the story of

John F. Kennedy's wartime exploits. It was made while he was in office. During that time I got to see a few real Japanese Zeroes and a bunch of PT Boats. The star of the movie was Cliff Robertson who would later win an Oscar for "Charlie." There was lots of excitement for a little kid with military attitudes and a longing to be a hero. Fortunately for all us little guys there was a pre-screening of the movie in Key West before release and I got to see it. I don't know that anything up until that time had made me feel so important. It wasn't long, then, until I would get to see the soon to be sainted man himself. John F. Kennedy was coming to Key West!

- - - - -

They say that there is always a breeze in the islands and that will mitigate the temperature. Could have fooled me. In July and August it's just friggin' hot! Even the breeze is hot! If you went swimming there was no cooling effect. The water was warmer than a bath you would draw in the lower reaches of hell.

One day we took all our plastic model fighter planes and B-17 bombers and decided to have a faux dogfight. We did this by pouring lighter fluid on the planes, which were placed on the ground in battle formation, and lit them on fire. Just how long can you look at your fighter planes sitting on a shelf doing nothing to protect anybody? The Americans always won and the carnage was fantastic. After it was finished all those model planes that cost fifty and 75 cents lay on the pavement like detritus from Pearl Harbor. It was horrible yet fantastic! No newsreel footage of the Japanese attacking us could compare.

There was a strangeness in the air with the adults. Something was going on but us kids couldn't quite figure it out. Their nerves were on edge and they didn't seem to tolerate us the same way. There were more planes and jets in the air. To the young mind this was way cool! Phantom jets on low streaking maneuvers were so overwhelmingly awesome! But, there were so many. Much, much more than there were before. One day, our president, John F. Kennedy, came on TV and announced a containment of the island nation of Cuba. And then the shit hit the fan!

Within days all of our neighbors were sent to the mainland. The presence of more jets and bombers became acute. The skies were black with weapons of mass destruction. Soon the Army and Marines sent down thousands of troops to protect the shores of Key West! The city ballpark was taken over by the army and it was filled with halftracks and tanks. Smathers Beach was dug up and turned into foxholes with machine gun nests just like in the John Wayne movies. Several street corners on Duval Street had ground to air missile batteries. The Russians were trying to ship missiles to Cuba and our president wasn't going to stand for it! The missiles already in place and those on the way were meant to be aimed at us. No kid, no adult was immune from the fear of the oncoming apocalypse. Lonely and frightened, because all my friends had been moved, I waited for the world to end as had been told me by the television news! But, as this went on, I continued to fish and trawl for shrimp with my butterfly net. I kept on making little battleships out of two by fours, setting them to sail and throwing rocks at them like I was some justified shore battery. One day a Phantom jet crashed because of mechanical reasons and the remaining people in the neighborhood all gathered to watch the pilot descend in his parachute. He landed on a small piece of land where I had accomplished all of my personal war games. He broke his back on landing but survived. We drove out in the family car to observe the jet's wreckage just a few yards from the shore. It was a scary time for a little guy like me. The Russians were coming and they wanted to change my life if not out and out kill me. I was nine years old. And I was very afraid.

The marina where the pilot had parachuted was one of my favorite spots to fish. I would go down to the docks and fish for snapper and barracuda between the docked boats. On the door of the entrance to the marina office there was a picture. It was of a man who had been skin diving but had been run over by the propeller of a boat. Across his back were four distinct marks where the propeller had hit him. In the picture he was sitting up trying to find some relief from someone where no relief was available. His cuts were six to seven inches wide and included a cut that almost severed his spine. It was gruesome and it was awful and why they posted the picture I will never know. I was told that this individual died from his wounds. From my view of the wounds I could only hope that he did, indeed, perish. That picture has stayed with me all these years!

The world was playing games with me. I didn't know up from down. My parents weren't the smartest people and I knew this at a young age. Who would protect me? Would I survive the oncoming debacle? I didn't know. I was a child and I was mostly interested in my model planes and fishing and exploring the hinter regions of this place that I knew of and explored and experienced in wonderment what the rest of the world called Key West!

Some people have very dark hearts. My stepfather possessed the darkest. The cruelty he administered to his family was of such a degree that the observer would have to cover his eyes, or leave, or stand up and do something about it. But that story isn't appropriate here. There are other dark stories and whether true or not they gripped my imagination as a young boy and gave me incredible nightmares.

At our house we subscribed to Argosy Magazine, Grit, and True Detective. On rainy days I would bury my head in them and learn about Japanese soldiers still fulfilling their obligations to the Emperor 15 years after the war had ended. I read about two-headed cows in the Midwest that gave birth to another set. Yet there was one story that was set apart from all the rest because it originated in Key West. Argosy had pictures of the whole lurid crime scene so I supposed it must have been true.

According to the story sometime in the late 50s or very early 60s a young man hired a deep sea fishing boat for a day's efforts at the catch. The crew consisted of the captain and his son. They motored out into the Florida Straits and proceeded to make their best efforts. I don't know if they were fishing for Marlin or Sailfish because the story is so far back in my mind. All I know is that the Coast Guard came upon the boat drifting later that day and found only the fisherman aboard. When asked about the crew the fisherman either had no answers or had created a slew of contradicting ones. It was then that the Coast Guardsmen aboard started noticing lots of blood yet no fish. Although fish blood was given in verbal alibi everyone seemed to know that something horrible had happened. As it turned out the fisherman was a maniacal killer who had murdered and dismembered his victims and threw the corpses, or what was left, overboard.

I don't remember this story from the papers at the time. I read it in an adventure magazine. Could have been pure fiction. I suppose I'll look up that story one day and see if it really does exist.

One time in our trailer park during our early stay there a family came in with a great big plywood box on wheels. It was probably twelve feet long by five feet wide. There were a husband and wife and two small kids. Even at my young age I supposed that they were Gypsies. I didn't even know what a Gypsy was, but I guessed, if you lived in a plywood box you must be one.

The father beat the wife and children mercilessly and many was the time that parents from the other trailers would come to put a stop to it. I remember the police showing up several times and taking the father away in handcuffs. He always came back meaner than ever. And then one day they were gone. They had no money and couldn't pay the trailer park fee. I never saw them again. About six months later my mother came to me to tell me that the whole family had been killed by a tractor-trailer ramming into them just before the Seven Mile Bridge. Much much later I saw the father again without the kids and wife. He had another plywood box and was parked on the side of the road by the Boca Chica Bridge and was chopping bait. We were fishing the same bridge. There were no children. There was no wife.

It was said by many of the Navy wives that the climate took its toll on marriages. I heard this discussion over and over again. With my mother and stepfather I knew this to be true because of all the pain they inflicted on each other physically. Some women in their frenetic states need the constant companionship of a strong man. If he isn't there then the companionship needn't be so devoted, the nearness of whomever will suffice. It got hot in Key West and the heat took its toll and left its scars. Sometimes you're a small kid living out some fairy tale existence on an island ninety miles out to sea with not a care in the world. Then darkness comes. Sometimes paradise is just another word for a bad dream.

WHAT TO DO

It's a morning of crystallized sunshine sparkling like a billion diamonds onto the tan on my face as I fish from the bridge.

The water is so very clear that the bottom is like regarding a magazine on a coffee table. There's about five snook down there along with one giant tarpon and a hammerhead shark. The whole crowd of 'em don't take to my silver lure that I move along in jerky movements but I'm still not gonna have old bait smell in my car. It's too unremovable and relentless on my poor sensitive sinuses. If the damn fish don't wanna bite I've said many times before that I really don't give a flip. This is my time with my God and my Zen spirits and sadly I must move way on down the road, if, for at least, a little while. I look off into the straits where on the other side Castro is just lighting his first cigar of the day and patting himself on the back for not letting people like me come over and visit Havana and have my Hemingway moment. Selfish old prick!

Two weeks later after having driven over a highway that can't be much more boring than driving the Russian steppes I'm taking a break from cleaning an old friend's refrigerator which has all kinds of articles in it long since un-namable and quite similar to some of the bait I refuse to carry in my car. It's a labor of love. A college friend of 30 years who has been in trouble with me, harangued with me, chased women with me but has stayed steadfast in devotion to a friendship that is more important to me than the near misses I've had with marriage. Presently I'm wondering where a 59-year-old might find meaningful work in an economy that doesn't include me. To leave those sobering thoughts I ponder over the weekend past where I met up with some more old friends and sang and listened to the best bluegrass performers in the land. This is what God has bestowed upon me and I gratefully accept and I sometimes look skyward and just smile in thanks for my maker knows I will never ask a personal favor.

Of course, being in such a hurry, I forgot blanket, pillows and sleeping bag but immediately ran into someone who not only had a bed in a camper but a queen size bed in a camper where I slept in dreams of catching the whopping tarpon on a six pound test line where I did not fight but let the large fish tire himself out over several hours. There's no need to dream of sexual exploits when one has the thought of a large fish on the line and he has all those diamonds shining in his eyes! The Zen in my dreams was the same as the Zen on my bridge and after a night of singing and jamming and having just a few beers I slept the sleep of a man contented with all that surrounds him.

By myself for a moment on a Saturday under an EZ up tent sitting at a picnic table and having a beer I was approached by an older woman who just began talking to me about what I'll never know and she went on and on and I feared she was crazed. She said her name was Guacamole McNulty and some of her diatribe was about some travel-rama she had been through but I just commiserated with myself about why someone would name herself that. Her mother certainly wouldn't. She asked me for a beer and before I could answer she went over to my car, opened it, and found where I had hidden my beer. She was good and I knew immediately that she had not only done this before but had been scoping me out for a while.

Gladly she didn't ask to borrow five or ten bucks or tell me the freedom she felt in letting her under arm hair grow as so many of these wanderers have done in the past. In junior college I took a canoeing class and got paired off with a fairly good looking woman in a bikini but who had hair growing out of every edge of the bits of cloth she was wearing. Not being a Deadhead I quit the class immediately by explaining I had an impending barber's appointment! I've lived in France and contrary to what many may have heard French woman (at least city ones) do not grow armpit hair down to their knees. And I was very grateful. Lucky for me my friends returned from the shower cabin and Guacamole McNulty went on her disturbed and crooked way. I locked my car.

The week before that I attended a Cajun/Zydeco fest where I knew a lot of friends would be in attendance. An old friend looked after me and we had some good conversations and I watched her work for no thanks at all and I wondered why she put forth so much effort. It was just her way and late on the second night I pulled two guitars out of my trunk and we played together for an hour and remembered things that we used to know and contemplated on things we might yet know.

During the day different people would approach me and tell me how much they didn't like this or that person and later one of those persons would approach me and say the same thing about the previous person or persons or about how important they were or about how less important the person was they were griping about in regards to different festivals we all attend. It was all too much so on the very second day very early I jumped in my car and went to visit my house, which I now rent out, and checked out the landscaping. It all passed my general inspection from the road so I just pointed my car in the general direction of my friend's house with the dirty refrigerator and hit the accelerator. That was the end of all the griping and the next weekend that was the end of Guacamole McNulty and whatever the hell she was talking about. Now I'm stuck with what to do and frankly I don't have a clue, don't care all that much and could just jump off the planet without a parachute if I were so inclined. Parachutes don't work in space anyway.

THE FIELD

It was after the festival and I was on my drive home. It seemed a good idea to take a detour and head on down through Kent to get the effects of summer in the west Connecticut woods.

The drive was pleasing. There was always a river on one or the other side of the road and fishermen with their fly rods and fishing vests were in almost every parking nook. The sun was only occasionally assaulted by a rogue cloud and shade trees provided an enthralling and pleasing aura to a mindless drive. At one point a very large bobcat crossed the paved road and slipped into the green underbrush. There was a dirt road in that direction that led I knew not where. Perfect! I had no schedule and a road to nowhere is the one I usually take whether real or imagined.

The gutted road led gradually downward until on all sides I was struck by the thunderous vision of wildflowers in multitudinous colors and numbers that struck me as almost bewildering to behold! I stopped the car and removed myself and gasped at the painting that God wished to envelope me in. Acres and acres of yellows and blues and reds that sashayed at times with the slightest of breezes. Behind me, down a steep cliff, flowed a large shallow river showing many rocks above the water against which the current splashed and started conversations with all the other parts of nature. It curved off in the distance in both directions shadowed by large oaks and walnuts right up to the water line.

There was no one near. If company was wanted or warranted it could only be someone in the romantic vein. You could share this vision with someone you loved or at least liked a lot without the disturbance of words or even breath. The sun shone, the water flowed in constant conversation, the trees guarded, and the flowers showed off in their own personal beauty pageant in a hideaway that is obviously little known.

For hours I stood or sometimes walked in admiration of a superior entity that could bring such quality to the visual and audial filament. I popped open a cold beer and scrambled down the cliff to soak my feet in the cool water and watched as birds fed and drank from the tumult. It was hours of a general detour that my maker provided for me and I will be ever grateful. Soon I will travel again down the long paved highway that leads me into an island habitat that also gives me strength because of the bounty of nature. I will always remember this field and in some way I hope the flowers and trees and river will remember me.

As time wore on I realized that the moment was meant for me but for only these short trials. I slowly and quietly closed the screen door of this large house and of what summer had provided for me and drove southward. All the flowers curtsied at my departure and the trees turned up their leaves. The river babbled goodbye and the bobcat once again crossed my path and appeared to be smiling!

THE PLAY

The play was written somewhat late in my lifetime by a person who would later only be known as The Author. The play concerned topics long since forgotten except for a part in the second and final act that came to define our age.

In the second act, initially presented in a large midwest city, there is a fight scene with swords with all the combatants being males enraged by some slight from someone not present and therefore no one to fight. But they begin to fight amongst themselves and it is the high point of the play. It became more so when one of the actors actually got a real and severely sharpened one and actually started chopping the other actors to pieces. Blood and body parts flew and it took some time for the authorities to separate the actors from the supposedly crazed perpetrator.

Although the public was shocked the trial was a sensation and almost all the witnesses exclaimed a modest hero worship for the defendant. Civilization as we knew it had been declining for decades and someone losing his marbles while acting with a real sword appealed to the public. Before the trial was over a new theatre had been found and a reprise of the play ensued. This time everyone was equipped with real and very sharpened swords and all were encouraged to use them. The bloodletting and mayhem were something awful but the public loved it. In a week's time the initial perpetrator was acquitted and the play went on for another seven performances with much killing, maiming and displaced body parts. The big star of the play was blood and people were screaming for it.

Legal entities were adrift as to what to do. The Supreme Court had tied the hands of the law so intricately that the law actually served as security during the performances. The public wanted blood and mayhem and that's what the public got. Soon the play was performed in half a dozen other cities with a command performance to come in Washington. When the play came to the capitol the Vice-President attended and was heard to exclaim that his "soul had been set free." The President locked himself in the White House not knowing how to handle the situation.

After six months the producers decided that the play would happen simultaneously in four cities across the United States. The blood and the killing were simply atrocious and it was an awful sight to see. But people were drawn to the color and wetness of the blood and soon all the actors were required to wear white togas so as to make the blood even more visible and satisfying. The rest of society remained normal and there were no outbreaks of violence in the streets. In fact the crime rate dropped drastically. In some large metropolises the phone at police headquarters never rang.

The President, after his initial nothingness, issued a proclamation that the play was legal and devoid of government intervention. Congress smelled a rat and demanded he rescind this order. They made the laws and how dare him delve into their territory? Then the Speaker of the House attended a performance and declared that he "had never been so refreshed in his life"! The President and Congress entered into a new era of good feeling.

The newspapers had a field day commemorating the end of American civilization while in the same breath praising the play for its inventiveness. The Catholic Church initially was against it but the hierarchy remained convinced it was no worse than what the Church itself had done in the middle ages. The Baptists protested but continued lynching blacks in the deep south. No one listened to them anymore. It seemed during this time that war or international transgressions were looked upon lightly. Who needed war? We got all the blood and guts we needed right here twice a night and a matinee to boot.

Soon vendors began showing up selling t-shirts with splattered blood drops on them. No matter how many they made they could never keep any in stock. You couldn't shop an aisle in Wal-Mart without running into someone with the blood splattered t-shirt. High schools started running the play themselves with drug-addled teenagers playing the important parts and the blood and gore continued unabated. In the meantime radical Muslims occupied the Holy Land and China took over Formosa. The French re-colonized Africa and a mad scientist took over the whole of Greenland. Americans didn't care. There was blood for everyone and body parts and gore to spare.

Finally there was a command performance for the President and the rest of the government. It happened in the spring with the blossoming of the Japanese cherry trees. Hundreds of thousands of citizens attended on the Washington Mall and it was announced that this would be an audience participation event. Swords were handed out to anyone over the age of ten and at the moment of climax during the second act any and all began swinging his weapon against his neighbor. The blood spillage and the chopping of limbs was like one huge Christmas party. Brother chopped brother and husband chopped wife. Blood ran as if a river into the Mall fountains. Body parts were stacked two stories high and the t-shirt concession made a mint. All was well in the world as far as Americans were concerned. Bliss reigned in the land for those who remained living and uninjured. It seemed as though there was gold on the horizon.

It had to end. There could be no doubt about that. The pivotal moment was an odd one to be sure but it galvanized the nation more than the play had.

Seems the Norwegians had taken to hunting whales off the New England coast again in defiance of international laws. Rednecks and tree huggers alike watched the newspapers aghast at the murderous intentions of our former allies. All of a sudden plugging someone with a sword and severing arms and legs and watching blood flow like champagne was not so interesting. "Save the whales" went the battle cry! And in one quick moment the play died like Steve McQueen in an Ibsen production.

The whales were saved and the Norwegians brought to order. We ignited a few wars just to keep the politicians happy and the President and congress renewed their animosity. Crime returned and the murder rate and robbery statistics rose. Gangs of outlaws roamed the land led in most part by one-armed bandits! And peace, as only Americans know it, returned to the land. The last performance of the play was held in Poughkeepsie just as

American destroyers sank the first Norwegian whaling ship. The Author, minus his left leg below the knee, retired to Key West and bought a charter boat. I hired his boat just last week and caught a dozen dolphin and several yellowtail.

Peace once again prevailed in its odd way across the land. You can still find some of the old blood spattered t-shirts in major league ballparks. They no longer cost an arm and a leg!

THE MUMBLERS

It's pretty hard on a party boat to please everyone on board. Some want to fish out on the reef and some would rather carouse around the mangroves. But if there is one single group you would hope for a spokesman so that the captain can make an educated guess on how to please the majority. You'd never expect everyone to speak up yet not be able to differentiate even one single distinct voice.

This is the group I met in a lobby at a popular resort hotel just off Duval Street. There was no particular leader to converse with but the front desk personnel pointed out a group drinking coffee and reading newspapers throughout the large room. There was a buzz in the lobby somewhat akin to Frank Zappa's 'dynamo hum.' I was expected to get them on a fishing boat for a half-day excursion. Try as I might I could not pinpoint a leader. Finally I decided to take control of the process and so climbed up on a divan and attempted to address the crowd.

Coffee cups and newspapers were cast aside in a noisy manner and the group approached me en masse. The crowd moved as one in tiny little steps much like the cartoon characters in South Park. There was an audible vocal sound being made by the whole group but no individual sounds could be detected. I explained the boat I had hired for them and where we would probably be fishing. There was a low groan from part of the assemblage and somewhat of a cheerful affect from the rest. The boat name and dock were given out and a time next morning to meet up. No one came up to ask a question on location. There were no queries as to the time or what to wear. They all shuffled off back to their coffees and newspapers as one. The din was featureless like small talk in church before the service begins.

After searching out the concierge I was finally directed to a middle aged portly fellow drinking tea and reading tourist pamphlets. He was the low-key leader of this group. I introduced myself and explained our boating trek for the day. He softly expressed his gratitude and we agreed on what dock to meet on the next day. But I was moved to ask who this group was. Seemed strange that no one stuck out in a crowd.

"That's the point," he said. "They work as a group."

"Doing what?"

"They are mumblers. They work for the movie and television industries. In westerns they are the people you see and hear in the saloons. They are always present at lynchings and usually they make up the posses. In courtroom dramas they are the audience, if someone is hanging from a ledge they are the crowd below. Their job is to mumble and make audible noises for the camera to capture. They are more or less 'extras.' "

"Never heard of that before."

"Every movie has them. Someone must make the ambient noise. In fact we're here because of noise or lack thereof. Our meeting here in Key West is to decide a course for ourselves in regards to the Screen Actors Guild. You see we are not allowed to speak, only mumble. If there is a part where someone says, 'hang him', or 'that's the one' or 'get him boys' it has to be a dues-paying actor from the Screen Actors Guild. We're here to protest that and plan a future action. And a little fishing."

"That's the weirdest thing I've ever heard. See you on the dock tomorrow." I called the boat captain and advised him to stock up on beer, vodka and ice. I explained what I knew and told him there appeared to be no worries.

The next morning at eight while I was helping the captain with loading the ice and beer 40 or so mumblers came shuffling down the dock. They were wearing shorts and tee shirts, some inscribed with 'BAG the SAG'. While almost everyone was involved in a conversation of some sort none could be made out. They could be talking about cold fusion or pornography but an outsider would never know. They boarded quickly as they were used to working as a group and the boat got underway. The captain had decided to fish the relatively shallow waters of the mangroves for snapper and grouper. There was no negative feedback. The mumblers stood as a group in the aft section some drinking coffee while others were having a morning beer. The sun was shining with a slight breeze out of the southwest. The noise level was at that of a quiet Catholic prayer with a couple of Allis Chalmer diesels in the background.

You never had to tell these guys to quiet down as there was no need. Most of the verbal noise was between the captain and his mate or one of the two and myself. After an hour some of the group had noticeably consumed a significant portion of the alcohol. They didn't get louder but did stumble a bit. The captain decided on a particular mangrove island that had a small sand beach and a large root system that snapper loved to feed in.

The mate passed out fishing rods and quickly everyone began fishing from the same spot in the aft section. They were like a school of mullet. You weren't going to separate them. But this was disadvantageous to the captain and mate who definitely had things to do during this excursion. The captain ordered the group to disburse throughout the boat. The mumblers could certainly take orders and soon they were all headed for the bow. This wasn't what the captain expected but these guys never did anything alone. So it came to pass that this significantly sized boat had 40 plus mumblers standing or moving slowly along the starboard rail. Almost 8,000 pounds of weight was on one side of the boat with no counterbalance to the port side. It also came to pass that the boat was swamped very quickly and settled in three feet of water with more than half of the company floating around the boat. It happened quickly. No one saw it coming. Dry one moment, wet the next.

The captain was mad, the mate was mad and I was plenty pissed myself. This was a quandary and wouldn't be rectified soon. We swore, we yelled, we screamed to high heaven. The mumblers mumbled.

The beer coolers, ice and vodka also made their way into the water and within a very short time the passengers and alcohol made their way onto the beach. Some of these guys were still fishing and some actually had fish on the line. The excitement was not palpable. These guys could have been tying their shoes. But no one drowned and everyone was quickly accounted for. The radio on the boat was dry and the captain went through his routine to save our souls. The depth of the water was the same level that was in the boat. The pumping and tow were going to cost a small mint. The quiet men on the shore were of no immediate problem as they were satiated with alcohol, the frequent snappers and the good weather but everything was going to change.

The captain made his call to the Coast Guard and once it was decided that no lives were in danger the authorities announced that they were tied up with three separate incidents of overloaded dinghies with Cubans trying to set foot on American soil. We were advised to hold tight while the auxiliary was contacted. On the mangrove the mumblers were finding their voices and coolers of beer kept washing up on the shore.

By midafternoon loud exclamations were originating from the sandy beach. I thought I heard someone say, "Stella!" A short time later I'm sure someone else said, "I coulda been a contender!" These quiet guys were quiet no more. "Here's Johnny!" "Houston, we have a problem." It was kind of funny. I popped a beer.

Over the next several hours the noise got louder and after a while a news chopper out of Miami hovered overhead. The mumblers threw full beer cans at it. Soon a few auxiliary Coast Guard craft had assembled just out of tossing distance from the shore. They awaited instructions from the mother service. "Edith, you Dingbat!"

"Gee, Wally!" It went on and on. Hey, the sun was shining and not a cloud in the sky but things were kind of getting out of hand. Little did we know that the news chopper had radioed in their story and soon the whole nation was aware of this 'quiet' multitude washed up on a deserted island with an endless supply of alcohol. No one was mumbling now. Out of nowhere one of the Cuban dinghies showed up with four or five wannabe Americans and they wanted to land their boat. Being on the back burner for so long the now inebriated mumblers welcomed the Cubans to their new island home. Cervezas all around.

Now it was an international incident and an embarrassment to the United States. Someone in the State Department was aware of the mumblers and suggested that the Screen Actors Guild be contacted. They also contacted the major film production houses. There were forty drunk extras and a handful of Cubans making America look bad. Intercontinental phone calls ensued for several hours.

Down at Fogarty's Bar on Duval Street a famous actor just happened to be having lunch with a girl he had met at a sex club the hour previous. He was making a movie in the middle keys and was taking a few days while the crew filmed some supporting scenes. His cell phone rang. "What?" And soon he was on a wave runner with his producer to a mangrove island full of ex-mumblers drunk out of their minds.

When the famous actor showed up just offshore on his WaveRunner a mumbler yelled, "You've got True Grit!"

Another screamed, "I'm outta order? You're all outta order!"

I had a few beers. I screamed, "I'm your wicked Uncle Ernie and I wanna fiddle about, fiddle about!"

The captain of the boat having given up on a quick rescue roared, "I'm not gonna hit ya, the hell I won't!"

It was a great party for the rest of the afternoon and one mumbler was heard to say, "I'm batman." The beer and vodka flowed, the famous actor came ashore and got lit. The sex club girl, on her own WaveRunner, came ashore and demanded her money. The Coast Guard finally showed up and just sat offshore awaiting instructions from anyone who could sort this thing out. Someone yelled out, "Lucy!" Someone else, "Rosebud!"

Everything got sorted out a few days later. The boat got pumped out and towed. The Cubans were returned to their homeland as the mangroves didn't count. The movie star was made to pay the sex worker. The production companies had to accept the mumblers as a specific union and one of their number could say, "lynch 'em" or 'that's my wife" during a movie production although they still weren't allowed on Broadway.

But to this day they come down in a group and do the Duval crawl once a year during the winter. If you listen closely at one of the intersections you can still hear the nondescript voices talking about who knows what about who knows where. And sometimes, just before closing time you can hear a mumbler yelling out, "On top of the world, Ma!"

SOMETHING OLD IN KEY WEST

One day in the fifth grade just after school let out at Sigsbee Elementary I noticed a lot of my classmates mulling around the tetherball pole talking in a serious way that seemed peculiar considering our age group. I wandered over and found out immediately that President Kennedy had just been assassinated. In that moment we were all grown-ups and very, very scared.

I had seen President Kennedy the previous Fall in his Lincoln Continental convertible somewhere along Truman Avenue. He was a handsome brave-looking man and I already knew of his exploits in PT-109 in the Pacific during World War II. To a ten-year-old kid he was way cool. He had come down to placate and congratulate us on our stamina and courage during the recent crisis. No matter what the media printed in the ensuing years I considered him a special and caring 'uncle.'

But after the crisis a kid's attention turned to things like fishing and building model airplanes and staying as far away from the parents who seemed intent on murdering each other. What was it in the weather that made two people supposedly in love turn on the other and inflict such cruelty? If the old man was away on military maneuvers and the old lady was in her cups I took off for the mangroves to catch fish or lizards or sort through the flotsam and jetsam of old sunken boats or lobster buoys. Sometimes I went with friends and sometimes I just went by myself. I didn't know who Huck Finn was but I was him. Every day was an adventure.

In those days the charter fishing fleet docked right up to Roosevelt Boulevard across from where the Ford dealership is today. Every charter had a huge nailed board where they would hang the day's catch. If you drove along the street on the way to the Tastee Freeze you could see thousands of pounds of Jewfish, grouper, red snapper, mutton, sharks, tarpon and yellowtail and so on. I always wanted to go on a charter but an article in Argosy magazine about that time slowed me down. There was a young man who chartered a boat, supposedly, and went out for a day's fishing with the captain and the captain's son. Sometime during the next day the Coast Guard found the boat adrift with only the angler aboard. According to the article the angler had killed the captain and his son and chopped them into little pieces. The authorities found the guy covered in blood with a few human remains still on the boat. My fantasy of going on a charter thereafter was null and void.

During this time a major studio decided to make a movie about Kennedy and his exploits during the war. You could see real PT boats offshore and the Japanese planes (which were US Navy trainers painted with rising suns) taking strafing runs. Most of that action took place up in the middle keys. I saw one of the PT boats again later in the Key West/Miami boat race somewhere off Stock Island. I never saw Cliff Robertson or Robert Culp, the stars, but there was a lot of neat World War II aircraft flying around. Down at the Strand theater on Duval, where Walgreens is now, I saw the world premiere of the movie. Before I saw this matinee the parents told me to be careful of guys touching my knee or offering me candy. THAT was scary! But I went with a group of kids and everything was hunky-dory. I never miss that movie when it comes around on reruns.

My friend Paul and I fished every day. At the marina on Sigsbee there was a dock where all of us barefoot fisherboys would cast for snapper or barracuda. One time I stepped on Paul's hook on the dock just as he was casting. That fairly large hook went so far up my foot that I believe I went into shock. My little boy logic couldn't figure out how that hook was coming out. Turns out it had to go further in my foot and then out following the direction of the curved hook and then cut with a pair of wire cutters. Don't want to ever do that again.

As a baseball fan I always had a baseball bat. I got them down at the hardware store on Roosevelt and it usually took a month of allowance to get one. I'd take rocks or pieces of coral and knock them into the empty apartments behind our building. I broke a lot of windows and frightened a lot of dogs but I was Huck Finn and I didn't care. Unfortunately there were a lot stickers that I had to remove from my socks and shoes and skin. They were not fun. The huge rain puddles and the waterspouts were fun. I liked being outside in a downpour.

Down behind the Poinciana School used to be a walled sports stadium. It was used for half-tracks and army trucks during the crisis. I played midget football there. It was in this place that I first had the wind knocked out of me. I thought I was dying. No breath would come. The coach came over and loosened my belt and stood over me until my lungs once again filled with beautiful wonderful air. I kept right at football into high school until I transferred to a Connecticut school that only offered soccer. What the hell was soccer? Well, at least I learned liberalism.

Sometimes at night I would sneak off to the marina with a flashlight and a fish net. My purpose was to catch the shrimp that would hang out in the seaweed near shore. If I kept at it I could get upwards of two pounds. Then I'd take it home to mom who would clean them and boil them in beer. Then she would make a tangy hot sauce with a mustard base. I've never been able to replicate that taste but it sure beat the hell out of cocktail sauce. She would also take my snapper catch and bread them and fry them with hush puppies filled with onions. Good times.

We had all lived through the crisis. The Russians were NOT coming. I lived every day like a kid without boundaries or until someone gave me some and beat the hell out of me for my forgetting. Then, in an instant, my president, our leader, the good uncle was shot dead on a Dallas street. What does a young boy do? Where is the trust? How does a ten-year-old boy figure in the great scenario of life?

He just keeps on keeping on. He lives his life. He remembers a great world leader who he had seen and who he will forever cherish. Then he goes fishing. Why not?

ALLIS CHALMERS

Allis Chalmers was a big breasted, full-bottomed 500 gallon tank of good times. When I first met her at the Parrot she was already over 70 years old. A good timing woman wrapped around a large beer she was bigger than life and she farted her way through an alcohol saturated night scattering customers and friends alike. One could call her a septic woman. And some did.

One night after a particularly gaseous Cuban meal she told me her life story up until that moment. I didn't catch it all as I had had flatulent food also and a ton of Cervezas. She started talking and I listened, more or less. Every once in a while we downed a shot of tequila and screamed rude stuff at the bartender. They didn't care. She was royalty.

When Allis was a young girl in Cleveland she was the homecoming queen at her high school. It didn't go over well. Her date had plied her with alcohol hoping against hope to get lucky and brag to his friends later. Ends up a lot of guys did some bragging and Allis Chalmers, the diesel of the party, decided it was time to leave town. Louisville, Birmingham, Pensacola and Tampa just got in her way. She landed, flat on her belly, on Smathers Beach in Key West, Florida sometime in 1959.

Being tightly packed and well endowed she got a job as a pole dancer in a club servicing the boys at the local naval air station. She was good and several musicians wrote songs about her and her seemingly wanton ways. Allis didn't like that. She was a good girl from a good family and she just went astray for a while. She turned down advances from every sailor and every man who made a proposal. She was a good girl in her own mind and she wasn't going to give it away. Then one day Dieter showed up.

Odd as it may seem Dieter was a survivor of a U-boat sinking during World War II off the coast of the keys. He lived in a little compound in the mangroves on one of the Saddlebunches. He sometimes came into town for some gardening work for cash and would frequent a couple of places for some good German beer. One night in a pole dancing joint he saw American sailors yelling obscenities at a precious young girl trying to make a few bucks and get home quick. A sailor named Bob Bair grabbed Allis by the legs and attempted to perform coitus right there in front of God and everybody. Dieter, from the Weimar Republic and the former National Socialist country of Germany, got off his barstool and beat the ever-living shit out of Mister Bair. He grabbed Allis from the stage, took her outside, and placed her on the handlebars and peddled her to his secret hideaway in the mangroves. She went along. Why not? It was a ten-mile ride.

When Dieter's U-boat had been sunk in 1943 he was 21 years old. In 1959 he was 37 and quite yearning for some female companionship albeit in a respectful manner. Allis wasn't sure about this island compound out in the mangroves and off the beaten track but she went along. After some time after they consummated their relationship they both decided to keep working although Allis would now being doing things differently and making a buck the honest way. They spent almost 30 years together and most of it was happy. They expanded the campsite always making sure that no one could ever find it.

They fished and they swam and they exulted in each other's company and they were grateful for each new sun shining day. They were a common item out on old route one fishing and crabbing in the flats. Sometime about five years before Dieter's death Allis assumed Keys Disease and began to drink her way to her demise. Dieter tried very hard to hold on to her but it was no use. Demon alcohol took hold and Allis went her own way. Dieter was left with his compound and his diary and his thoughts of his homeland and a useless war and what was left of his life. I found him there some years later.

Ms. Chalmers made her way back to the main island and started a new career or two. Sometimes she turned tricks. Sometimes she bartended. She smoked a boxcar of pot and snorted a trunk full of cocaine. She was a wreck sometimes and sometimes she was most exquisitely beautiful. But time took its toll. One day she woke up and she was a troll. She got a job as a gardener and plied that trade for many years. She was a great big pillow of a woman and she enjoyed life in a way that most mothers would not approve. I met her in the later years.

The Key West Police knew Allis Chalmers well. She had spent some time in the county slammer for various semi-minor infractions. But she always had clean clothes and makeup But, man, she loved her booze!

I met her about 1985 or '86 in the Parrot. She had already eaten her standard fare of yellow rice, and Cuban boiled chicken with curry and green peppers. I sat next to her and ordered a drink and stretched my arms, which unfortunately caused her to spill her drink and make a big ruckus because of it. She stuck her face in mine and demanded a new one. At the same time all that Cuban food and cooked peppers had all coagulated and fermented to such a degree that the lower intestines decided that it was time to expel. Expel they did, all to the discomfiture of the clients at the bar. Every cigarette and every lighter in the act of lighting suddenly brightened to two exponents of the sun while a fume close to that of a sewage treatment plant permeated the environment. Ladies and gentlemen, Allis Chalmers has entered the room!

Well, she blew that room away! Things sometimes got better during the evening, but, you know what? It got worse again. Then someone with a cell phone ordered out for baked chicken and peppers to be delivered to the bar. Allis may have shit her pants! Not sure. There was lots of good fresh air on the walk home.

A huge diesel truck pulled up beside me. Driver asked me if I knew Allis. Do I know Allis? Yeah, I know Allis. She's down on Whitehead Street having a good time and making an ass of herself. Just another lost soul who came to paradise, saw the sights and lost her heart. Then finally lost her way. She wouldn't be the last.

JOE BEANS

For Joe Beans its diatribe time. It's about seven in the morning at a concrete picnic table at Higgs Beach. The loonies are all awake. Most have not taken their meds. Besides, most of the psychotropics can be traded in on several bottles of booze.

"Kill all the niggers and faggots and Catholics," Joe begins. "Swimminy gotomee, need a frontal lobotomy. Pantywaists, that's what they all are. Ridin' girls bikes. Pie. I like pie. Sweet pie. Sweet pie is the best. Can't be ridin' girls bikes. What's the world comin' to? Beer, beer, need a pap smear. Pantywaists ridin' girls bikes. Beer and panties on girls bikes. Its the liberals, they're doin' all the damage. Wearin' them panties. Red ones. The best kind. Ya gotta ask yerself did I fire six shots or only five. Huh? Punk! Catholics started the Crusades. The Pope said kill a Muslim and get a free pass to heaven. The Pope on a girl's bike sniffin' panties. Red ones. Good Pope. Here boy, fetch."

A Deputy Sheriff drives up next to the picnic table. This particular law officer is ample. More than ample. He is a team inside of one large uniform. He decides to address Joe Beans from the safety and comfort of his air-conditioned vehicle without any of that unnecessary exercise.

"Joe Beans, you been drinking in public again?"

"Drinkin', thinkin', doin' a lot of stinkin'. Christmas comin'. Santa is a pantywaist ridin' girls sleighs. Lazy days, lazy days, takin' the sun's rays."

"Now Joe, we got some complaints yestidee 'bout you drinkin' beer and pissin' all over the beach. Ya tryin' ta git some baloney sandwiches down to the jailhouse?"

"Whore house butt fuckers fast finger guitar pluckers. I got me a dream. Judge a man by his character and not the color of his skin. Santa's comin' to town. Get down on it."

"Well, Joe Beans, brother, if I have ta come back again I'm gonna havta arrest ya. You savvy'?"

"Savvy savvy pooped my platty!"

Then Joe Beans walks down the street in no particular direction. He follows a chicken for a while somehow formulating a patchy thought about chicken wire and the correlation of its design in comparison to the lost synapses and former tabernacles that used to be his brain. He knows he's nuts and he knows there's not a damn thing he can do about it. He sees a purse next to a park bench beside an older retired woman. It's in his shirt no muss no fuss and no one the wiser. Out on the beach again he counts his newfound cash and lobs the purse in the water. He didn't even think to search for meds.

Thirty-three bucks. Got me thirty-three bucks, monkey on my back and the president sucks! Dance a little jig, gonna eat me a fig. Goddam Pope and his panties. Maybe a G-string. Pope in his G-string. Drinkin' some beer with some panties on. Parties on!

Joe Beans walks down the street He's an average-size guy although a little stooped. He has no shirt on. He's got tattered long pants and something that used to be called shoes. His graying scraggly beard is about a year old. Bugs live in there. Sometimes birds want to check him out for nest materials. The other bums turn their noses up at him. He's got a twelve pack and he's back at the picnic HQ with $22 to spare. Life is grand.

Look at the guacamole on that holy! By Jesus she'd look good in red panties and a Santa hat. Antonia, Antonia, why Macedonia? Boats, boats, everywhere boats. I ate a boat once. Many parts of the pinecone are edible. Read it in the Bible. Cell phones on a moped. How ya do dat? Homer Simpson likes beer. Beer, beer, happy New Year. This table looks soft and cuddly. Wish I had panties. Red ones. Put 'em on my head and go to sleep on this nice soft Posturepedic losodedic.

Three cruisers pulled up and the officers, all buff and fine tuned pick Joe Beans off the table and put him in the back of one of the cars. He was transported to County Detention where he would spend the next few nights and get just a bit more than baloney sandwiches. After the first night the employee known as the county psychiatrist made Joe Beans take the medication that he had long known to administer to this lost soul and our hero became as sane as the Speaker of the House. Joe was given three days medication, his $22 and set loose with a new Goodwill outfit and shoes. He set off for the Parrot. This is where we usually met. The county always called me when he got out of jail.

He was clean-shaven with a nice haircut. He had had several good hot meals and most importantly he was on his meds. He had three days worth. That was three days of sanity for one of the most beautiful human beings I've ever met. No one ever offered more than three days worth of meds because history had shown they all got sold in deference to liquor. "How ya doin', Joe?"

"I'm good. Sorry I haven't been around for a while but apparently I also live this other life."

"That you do, Joe."

"I'm sorry. And I'm also glad you came by. Did you hear from my daughter? Are the grandkids all fine?"

"Everyone's good, Joe. They miss you. You know I keep an eye out for ya."

For the next hour Joe and I quaffed several beers. I wasn't going to lose him because he was on his meds. Right now he was a sober guy having a few beers and he thought of himself as normal. I thought of him as normal. No point in discussing the raging lunatic alcoholic in his other self. He knew of that guy but didn't know him. The talk as always reverted back to his three tours in Nam. He survived the entire siege of Khe San. Anyone knows about that knows that that is saying a lot. After the battle the marines just abandoned the camp and airfield. Joe never got over that. Over 200 marines died there. For what? For what indeed.

We stretched our conversation into small talk and sometimes politics and the stock market and even the jobs situation. A totally sane and coherent human being. I felt sad when I left. He had two more days of meds which I knew he would take. Then, fighting all the way, he wandered down into the black tunnel unmedicated and immune to everything cognizant.

Bananas, bandanas. I love bananas. Pudding too! Great oogly moogly look at that piece of tail. Tail, tail shot a quail. Charlie Brown's Christmas. Yeah. Ding dong dingin' we be sing, sing singin' a song. Ho, ho, ho. Git that lizard offa my bed. Lizard, lizard gonna eat the gizzard. Oh happy day. For the benefit of Mr. Kite there will be a show tonight on trampoline. Lean, lean dancin' machine. Ooh, a purse. Gotta make hay while the sun shines.

The sun came up. The sun went down.

GOURMAND IN PARADISE

You can get great food in a lot of venues. Some hamburger joints are to die for. The chain stores not so much. After winning $12,000 once at Mohegan Sun I took my buddy Tony to the Morton Steak House in Manhattan.

I was overwhelmed with the quiet ambience but also the famous and near famous necking in the dark booths with their girlfriends. There were lots of them but it was a large room. The waitress brought us cocktails but did not offer a menu. We made it clear we were beefeaters and so she left us for a while to do some exploratory with the chef. Another waitress made sure our drinks never got dry. There were some big names getting some small favors under the tables. The third round didn't suck either.

After a while our original waitress came back pushing a very large three-tiered cart. On the top shelf there were Kansas City steaks two inches thick wrapped in clear plastic for our view. Our combined views saw meat of a quality and freshness and redness that brought us into a sexual excitement. On the second tier was lobster, oysters, shrimp and so much seafood it would be impossible to describe. The third tier, at eye level, had prime rib, roast beef the color of the sunset and pork chops three inches thick. World-class eating!

Years later someone asks me about eating conch. What does it taste like? They asked using the 'ch' sound rather than the hard 'k'. We're talking tourists here. And they want to eat conch! I'm asked again what it tastes like. You're kidding, right? We're in Key West and they serve El Salvador conch. Can't harvest conch in the United States anymore. And you eat it why? It's a Goddam slug!

So I told them about my view on eating conch. I prefaced my remarks in the appropriate fashion leading the learner to the altar of my argument. Remember this:

You're in the 4th grade in Bunghole Elementary. It's the middle of winter. The heat is turned up to a furious degree and the temperature is provided by those old steam radiators that burglars like to steal now. Everyone is nearly asleep from the heat and lack of moisture in the air. The teacher's only awake because of the pint of K-Mart perfume she slapped all over her body before she left the house. She was a hefty woman and thought people might smell her body odor. It certainly kept her awake and fought a tough battle with the urinal cakes in the boys' lavatory.

Over in the front row by the windows Johnny Smart is picking his nose. He has a problem with inarticulate particles collecting on the hairs in his nostril. Everyone has. Johnny Smart has caught onto a big one. It has a little moisture and the more he moves it around the more it collects lollygagging nose junk. Pretty soon there's a pretty giant buggar just waiting to be introduced on stage. Johnny takes his cue and pulls it from his face. He extends it in front of himself and admires it like he just caught a butterfly. He takes one quick peek around the room and sticks the item in his mouth.

Johnny Smart would one day win the Medal of Honor, two silver stars and two purple hearts for outstanding heroism during several episodes in the Ia Drang Valley. He jumped on a grenade to save his buddies but it didn't go off. He saved several chopper pilots from burning to death after their crafts had been shot down. He lived in a humid environment which caused his nostrils much inflammation and much to the consternation of the guys in his outfit always had his finger up his nose. Years earlier he had consumed the material that had collected there in a room full of people. Unfortunately I saw the whole thing. A young boy eating sniveling material with the consistency if not the flavor of a rubber band. Oh my Christ!

That's what conch tastes like. So I'm told.

WHAT I SAW

Mindlessly driving out of the main island on a side street I was diverted from my endless daydreams by a woman walking down a little used sidewalk.

She was tallish and blond, wearing a deep cranberry red ensemble of skirt and blouse with a brisk step. Although the skirt was mini and much admired by these eyes it wasn't too short. The legs, although thickish at first, were of a woman who worked out a lot. She didn't overdo it. The behind didn't stick out like a hot air balloon on a Sunday sail and the breasts were just a tad more than informative. Her step was mellifluous and quite agreeable. There was no suggestion of the left tackle returning to the huddle in her gait and this conferred upon her an angelic repose infused with education, determination and intelligence. She was gone in a flash.

I continued on and stopped at a local quick mart for a coffee. As I stepped out with my steaming brew there she stood, an Isis on an island, just closing up her cell phone. There was no thought pattern to deal with, I had to address her then and there. Opportunities are to be taken advantage of.

"I noticed you walking down the street a few minutes ago. I thought you were beautiful." I waited the slap, the denunciation, the insult.

"Thank you," she said, "you've made my day."

So for the next ten minutes we spoke of many things and who we were. She was a graduate of the Rhode Island School of Design and was a graphic artist. Damn, I had friends that went there who were overly intelligent but never crammed that info down my throat. I kind of looked up to them. Here, in my paradise reverie, I was conversing with a lovely beauty with direct eyes and firmness and she didn't treat me like I was coming on.

Of course, knowing that she knew I wasn't coming on, I couldn't come on. There was a Mexican standoff in my brain. Nothing could be done except for sweet conversation. As the talk ran on I spoke of where I lived and where I fished on my favorite bridge and so on. She told me about her family, an ex-boyfriend and her vacation in the keys. After a short while it became apparent that I should go. There were no instigating suggestive remarks. We said our goodbyes. I watched her walk off in that most desirable tablature of legs to sidewalk and imprinted in my mind the most wonderful woman I had ever met. Then she was gone.

As always I take some time out to fish on the bridge most days. Seldom do I catch anything as I use a lure instead of bait. I don't want to catch snapper or small grouper and get involved with all the cleaning. Small edible fish are like air molecules down here and if I wanted snapper I could buy it at the supermarket already cleaned and ready to cook. I want a trophy fish. You never know when one might swim by in these shallow waters but you have to be ever vigilant. Besides, my personal Buddha resides in the sky and on the water surface when I cast. Never cared whether I caught anything or not. A good smoke and a cold beer with my line in the water is always enough. Get rid of the shirt and I've got a good tan going.

Over to the left a silver Mercedes pulls up to a parking spot. It just sits there for a few moments while the sun envelopes the world in its embrace. Then, just then, an entity exits the vehicle and familiarity resounds. The girl with the deep red cranberry outfit, just as before, emerges with all the grace of a Queen of Monaco. It's my fantasy woman and she's walking towards me. My legs turn into Velveeta cheese.

She walks onto the bridge and approaches me. She says nothing. She puts her left arm around my head and draws me near. She puts the lips made of rose petals and red wine next to mine and gently caresses my hips with her other hand. Her tongue just vaguely touches mine yet an innate sensation of lust overwhelms me. I only move my hands in a way to differentiate whether there's panties or a thong. Got to slow down here or ruin this whole Penthouse moment. We have several moments connected in this way. I am entwined with this cranberry red gift of the gods and she sure seems to be liking me. At one point she suggests that we return to my house and continue on for the rest of the day. One can only acquiesce.

The rest of the day is not something I can reasonably speak of in a gentlemanly way. Some things are private and not meant for common dissemination. Sometimes a guy just gets lucky and he has to deal with it. As those sweet lips massaged mine and those hands began to explore I simply lost my mind and went deep down into one of Alice's excessively figurative rabbit holes.

Of course after the second paragraph this story never happened. It was just a good day of fishing. Much love to all my fishing friends!

I CAN BELIEVE THAT

Where's the money? There's never enough money. I scurry around doing painting jobs and odd jobs and whatever such!

And listen to the radio. Here's what I heard on the radio: A woman in Argentina wanted her husband to pay explicit attention to her. She wanted something in the oral vein but she also wanted to kill her husband. She planted a sort of poison in her va-jay-jay. Things get better.

The husband, kind of liking that sort of thing, went to the shores of bliss. Unfortunately he smelled something in the toxic arena and decided he was smelling a rat, so to speak. He grabbed his wife by the hair, threw her in the car, and drove off to the hospital. Seemed sensible. At the hospital everyone smelled a rat and called the police. The woman called her lawyer. He showed up and said, "Keep your lips sealed!" You can't make this shit up!

On the bridge I fished for nothing for the 29th day. Didn't matter. Catching the fish is not the end point. It's all about the Zen moment. The local osprey flew over and laughed at me. He had a two-pound snapper in his claws. I had nothing. He just kept laughing. I popped a beer, lit a smoke and flipped him the finger. A couple of F-18s flew over. I felt safe.

A young woman in a string bikini came by and struck up a conversation. She certainly was nice. I wanted to reach out and talk about the world. I created conversation to see how that went but the Argentine woman came to mind. I wanted to discuss things sexual and personal but the South American va-jay-jay put that to bed. I made a few more casts on my rod and decided to end my fishing day. I've had worse thoughts on any given bridge. The osprey flew over and laughed. He had another fish. I didn't.

I went out with my friend Flo last week and we put a bottle cap on our night. The Bottle Cap was the name of the palace where we ended up for last drinks. It wasn't a palace, just a place for last drinks. And that's what we had. Last drinks. Last rites! Nice beautiful people around us and yet I can't remember even one. I'm sure we struck a chord also. I don't need a fish, I don't need a poisoned va-jay-jay. I think I've been there before. Aren't there better ways to murder your husband?

In the morning the wind blew out of the northeast. The osprey stayed home. The bikini chick never showed and I lost my lure on a piece of mangrove sticking out in the middle of the canal. I'm pissed about a lot of things up north but my lips are sealed! I'll do it again tomorrow.

FULLY

Fulgencia Batista III, known to his friends as Fully, lay on his back semi-enjoying the sun shiny day and the slapping waves. There could have been more enjoyment, even merriment if his current predicament could be changed ever so slightly.

The night previous Fully had entertained several ladies whom he had just met at the Bottle Cap Lounge. They were blonds in their mid-30s hailing from some small town in Connecticut. It was nice to think now with the sun shining and the waves slapping that he might have carved out a ménage à trois with the lovely entities and regale his friends later with his sexual prowess. But his friend Jack, also from Connecticut, seemed to get the upper hand and was last seen around 11:00 herding his new conquests down Duval Street. What an asshole! Fully got it in his head to get down to a local tourist shop the next morning and order a hundred pins printed with "Jack's an Asshole" and pass them out to all their mutual friends. Imagine that jerk coming into the Bottle Cap and everyone is wearing one of those pins. Serve him right.

But, as things, turned out, he had to work the next day on the shrimp boat with Captain Matty. The shrimp didn't run like they used to but a chilly day with a northeast wind in February was one day that they did appear. Making bucks was much more important than feeding his libido. The hell with women! There's always tomorrow. Well, there might be a tomorrow. The sun shone. The waves slapped.

Fully didn't have a whole lot to worry about as he was a seasoned sailor. This current predicament could be handled relatively easily. But it was a predicament. The shrimp boat, aged as it was, always took on water and the electric pumps ran continually. But when the Carnival Cruise Line ship, the Triumph, ran by at thirty knots the wake swamped the little fishing boat and it sank in three minutes. Captain Matty got one life raft and Fully the other. The cruise ship captain had no idea he had swamped a shrimp boat and so headed off to its inevitable destiny. If Fully had known that within a few short hours the ship would suffer a fatal engine fire and the staterooms would be flooded with human sewage he might have gotten some satisfaction. But Fully had a destiny also and it wasn't looking too good.

Floating in a rubber raft 25 miles out in the Gulf Stream wasn't an impossibly bad place to be. Ship and fishing boat traffic was usually heavy. Usually. Where's a Goddam ship when you wanted one? Oh well, it was just a matter of time. There were two kinks in the armor. Captain Matty's raft had disappeared to the north and Fully's had taken a decidedly bad drift to the south. The Gulf Stream is not just one gigantic climate changing current but a conglomeration of many dozens of currents going in all kinds of directions. It generally ran through the Florida Straits into the Gulf of Mexico but tributaries ran off to Central America, the Caribbean and Cuba. Cuba! Goddam Cuba? Goddam that Jack! If I had stuck to my guns, thought Fully, I'd be in bed with two blonds, a hangover and would have missed work. Cuba?

By 1959 Havana had become an American mafia bastion. The Gambinos and the other New York and New Jersey families owned all the casinos, half the hotels and most of the restaurants on the Grand Boulevard. It was a pit of iniquity run by crooks and the general Cuban public be damned! The mafia ran the whole island it seemed and American justice couldn't do a thing about it. Just one big self money-laundering organization free of taxes with the inmates running the asylum. But, up in the hills there was this guy Castro who didn't care for this arrangement, and so, he and his boys started knocking off crooked policemen and fighting with an army who only wanted to get down to the casinos every night, have a few drinks and maybe find a prostitute.

In Castro's mind everything would be great if he could just get rid of 'el presidente.' Then he could shove all the gangsters out and create an island utopia. In those days Castro was thought of as a savior. No one knew that one day he would hang his real clothes out to dry in the climate of communism or that he would harangue Khrushchev into dropping the 'big one' on Florida just 90 miles away. That Khrushchev had a much cooler head and decided not to destroy the world is a whole other story. But what Castro wanted in 1959 was to rid the island nation of immoral influence and that jackass Batista!

He did a damn fine job of it. One day the dictator looted the treasury and scooted out of Havana on a mafia-owned aircraft and made habitation elsewhere. Castro and his insurgents were in town twenty minutes later. He changed the country dramatically and he and Che Guevara were national heroes. One of their first acts was to put a price on the head of Fulgencio Batista and all of his descendants. It's the Latin way. Wipe them off the map. Of course, if you're Fulgencio Batista the 3rd, drifting about 60 miles off the coast of a country where your name is like a deadly cancer, things could look a whole lot better. Fuck that Jack. What an asshole!

Captain Matty was picked up by an excursion boat on its way to the Tortugas. He of course told the boat skipper about his mate and his drift pattern and the Coast Guard was summoned. He then had a beer and a sandwich and decided to enjoy himself on this free trip out to the very last Key. He regaled the passengers with his exploits and was fed a continuous supply of beers by this guy Jack in the company of two blonds. It was a beautiful day!

Fully was thinking the same thing. It was a fine day. Not too hot, a good steady breeze, gently lapping waves. It was just, that by looking at the sun, he could see that now he was closer to Cuba than he was to Stock Island. Oh well, the Coast Guard would be looking for him now. He had a gallon of water and several Snickers Bars. This part of the ocean was a busy place. He'd be picked up soon.

Unknown to Fully was that there was a weird convention in town that consisted of a bunch of guys who called themselves 'the mumblers.' These were guys used as extras in the movies and television and just made a lot of background noise to give the story a bit of reality. They were in Key West to do a little fishing and make some plans to unionize their group. A lot of them wore t-shirts that said, "BAG the SAG" in reference to the Screen Actors

Guild who refused to give them any lines in any production. They could only make background noises. As a group they were pissed off. In terms of Fully they were presently extremely intoxicated, stranded on a sandbar and usurping all the resources the Coast Guard could muster. As a matter of fact their stranding had become an international incident. A rubber raft with a descendant of the last dictator of Cuba was the last thing on anyone's mind. Getting the drunk and increasingly infamous mumblers off that sandbar was job one!

After twelve hours on his raft drifting at the rate of 5 knots an hour Fully saw the outline of the coast of a country he had never known. Fully was born in Miami to his mother Tina and a no account father. Tina had been born to the ex-dictator in one of the countries where he would claim asylum. She didn't know which. She never knew how she got a passport or how she ended up in Miami. She would never be able to fathom or pass down to her son that an American blackjack dealer by the name of Johnny, recently removed from Cuba by the revolution, had acquired her passport by devious means on Martinique sometime in the early 70s. She also didn't know, and indeed didn't need to know that Johnny was the father of Jack the asshole who in the present day was chatting away with a shipwreck survivor and two blonds from Connecticut while on an outing to the fort on Dry Tortugas. Such is life.

Bumps to the raft were becoming annoying. It wasn't like lapping waves. Fully took a peek over the side and was startled to see a school, a herd, a crowd of ten foot bull sharks. Oh shit! Then a motorized craft of some sort could be seen in the distance. It wasn't coming his way but it did appear to be patrolling. Patrolling could only mean a government craft. There was only one government allowed to patrol in these waters. For the first time in his life Fully wished that his last name was Smith! Considering his present circumstances his name was Shit! He consumed his last Snickers bar, laid his head on the side of the raft and stared at the rising moon. Light, like his last candy bar disappeared into an abyss.

On a sandbar in the lower keys the chaos with the mumblers was being sorted out. There were now elements of the Coast Guard available for other duties. The guy on a rubber raft was an option but there was a cruise ship in the gulf leaking sewage all over every which way that had lost steerage and had about three thousand very pissed off passengers. The Coast Guard, like the Lone Ranger, went off to the rescue. The moon rose higher over the Florida Straits. A very frightened man with an unfortunate last name awaited his fate and probably his doom. Ah, but life is fickle. You just never know what might happen.

Flying at about five thousand feet in a seaplane as big as a Greyhound bus, rescued from the U.S Navy wrecking ball, was a man humming a song and wanting to do some fishing. He was a wealthy man and if he wanted to put down to fish, well then, he damned well would! He had just performed a free concert on Duval Street in Key West and before the first autograph seeker found him he was up in the air and out of Margaritaville before you could shake a stick. And thank God. Another few minutes and that asshole Jack would be pestering him to record one of his shit awful songs. You just gotta love a seaplane. You're up and gone! Gotta do some fishing. Now!

Fully understood that all he had left now was a half-gallon of water and a filet knife. On the negative side he was surrounded by hungry bull sharks and sitting just a few miles off the Cuban coast with the worst possible thing he could own: his last name. Suicide was an option. He didn't know what the authorities would do with him. No way they were ever going to believe he came here as a shipwreck survivor. He could only be here to foment a new revolution. There were plenty of people who liked the ex-dictator. There was a good argument that the grandson could cause a stir. Of course being caught meant the firing squad. They weren't going to send him back. They got rid of all the whack jobs in the Mariel Boatlift. He was a political prize. Ah, who would ever put two and two together? Hmm, should I ditch the wallet? Just then a bull shark gave the raft a good knock. Scary enough. And wouldn't you know it there goes that rich bastard in his flying boat. Bet he's singing 'Havana Day Dreamin.' Fucking Jack!

On the cruise ship urine was running down the bulkheads in torrents, rivers, maelstroms. To make matters worse the crew started giving out free cold beers. Beers! Who knows what evil lurks in the mind of the shadow? As all the lavatory systems were dead and completely deceased the visitors on this ill-fated voyage had decided amongst themselves to figure out a bathroom situation according to the sexes. It was almost unanimously decided that the women would use the aft section of the ship and the men would partake of the bow.

The ship was by now undertow and there was a measurable headwind. And so it came to pass, both figuratively and literally that the first three hundred men to relieve themselves of the free beer and good tidings from the crew, pissed into the wind and thus and therefore pissed into their own faces, shirts, pants, shoes, etc. A fact, that had Fully known, would have appreciably improved his mental outlook. Free beers and the shitters don't work. Can't make this stuff up.

One thing about a bull shark. He's got patience. One thing about a survivor adrift in a life raft. He's scared shitless! Fully pulled the filet knife from its sheath. If both wrists were cut immediately there would be no time to panic. Inevitability would take its very fast course. That time was approaching. Or the time to surrender to the bull sharks. Or the firing squad. But, who knows, maybe Castro's brother is a much nicer guy. The damn lunatic in his seaplane just circling a few miles away and I know he doesn't even see me. And there goes that patrol boat again. Man, two blonds and all night on my hands. I shoulda said something. He felt the knife for its sharpness. Not quite there but it would have to do.

When Fidel Castro took over in Cuba he pretty soon made it abundantly clear that he was a communist. President Eisenhower got together with his CIA cronies and planned a counterattack from Cuban Americans residing in Miami. Eisenhower would never get the chance to carry out his plans. That was left to the next president. Too bad the next president held back on promised air support. Castro foiled the attack and all the survivors were jailed for the next two years. When the survivors returned the majority were made to go to Viet Nam as payment for their freedom. One of those not freed was Fully's no-good father. He was shot immediately. No trial. No news headlines. Just a casualty of war.

In the dark, the seaplane landed somewhere near Cuba's twelve-mile limit. The engines were shut down and the tarpon poles were retrieved from the hold. The moon, not full, still registered plenty of night. The rich guy and his co-pilot retrieved a few beers from the cooler. They stuck a CD in the stereo. The pilot listened to himself. The waves lapped. The moon shone.

Captain Matty was beginning to figure things out. Wasn't this Jack guy the asshole that Fully told him about this morning? The guy seemed innocent enough. Could chat it up with the best of them. But somewhere, deep down this dipshit had a cold heart. Captain Matty began to warm to Fully's idea, mentioned at sunrise, that he was going to make a bunch of "Jack's an Asshole" pins and then distribute them down at the Bottle Cap. True Justice. He was showing off the chicks like he was Hugh Hefner or something. Asswipe! I hope Fully's okay.

The patrol boat was definitely coming his way now even though it was dark. No way this rubber raft was showing up on radar. Didn't matter, here it came. The first filet knife cut down the wrist was quick and easy. There was no pain. The sudden jerk on the raft made him think that the sharks had thrown out all caution and were about to sit down to Thanksgiving dinner. He felt that he was moving faster than before and this could only be attributable to ensuing death. Damn the raft was moving fast! Blood spurted up and down his arm and over the raft.

Not what you want with sharks near. But, what did it matter? Life was something for the past. Fully lost his vision and then his feel. He never heard the machine gun mounted on the patrol boat fire a warning shot across his rubber bow. The dark became darker.

****

Sitting in Key West harbor just off Mallory Square sat an old Navy seaplane with its nose into the wind anchored to the bottom. On the square there was a dilapidated old Frenchman doing a show with his trained cats. "No, no," he said, "no videos, pictures only." Some college guys were puking in an alley after consuming too much vodka and inhaling, inhaling if you can believe it, Cuban-seed cigars from Costa Rica. Their girlfriends played on their cell phones. Fully checked his bandage and took another swig of his Sharkfin beer. He had been a fisherman all of his life and he never heard of anyone catching a life raft with a shipwrecked sailor on it. You gotta love the cosmic aura. Before he left the seaplane the captain gave him a copy of his newest recording on CD. Too bad, Fully was a Travis Tritt fan. But, hey, the guy's fishing for tarpon and he catches me. What a life. Despite all of his travails of the previous day Fully walked over to Duval and at the first tourist shop ordered 100 pins that said, "Jack's an Asshole". Then he went to the Bottle Cap.

MUNCHING

(AN APOLOGY TO A FRIEND)

Deep in the dark night resides a man with a challenge on his mind. Find some food whatever its taste and chomp down hard.

At one point I saw this woman sitting catty cornered to me talking to her friend. I had been to a specialty tequila bar and had imbibed from its wares. Presently I was somewhere else looking catty cornered at a lovely woman while talking with friends. My eyes were beginning to hurt. The time had come to act. Jeez, Yogi, what'll we do now?

I went over all bravelike and such. I said, "Remember in 6th or 7th grade and your girlfriend said that her other best friend had said that your friend (meaning you) was cute? Well, that's why I came over. I needed to tell you that." I did not offer to buy her a drink nor did I stick around for conversation. That was that. I knew immediately that I had her respect. Our eyes touched a few more times in the next hour and finally her team left the premises. I had another tequila drink.

On my walk back to Flo's house I thought about that a lot. That and how far Flo's house was from where I was. But we stopped again, ole me and Flo, and ducked into this martini place where I only wanted to eat some of their stuffed olives. Olives with such a rich and entreating aura with a taste made somewhere south of Naples or maybe Athens. Really great Goddam stuffed olives! Here we met a couple where the husband was an executive at Longines, the timekeeping and watch-making company from Switzerland and his wife from Meriden, Connecticut. They knew each other from childhood and eventually married. I never got over the girl from Meriden marrying a guy from Switzerland that worked for Longines. It was incongruent.

Well we had some stuffed olives and I believe some red wine. Then we talked about places where we had been mutually in Europe. Perpignan came to mind. He knew what he was talking about and so did I. Just great, pleasant people. Somehow Flo and I got home. I believe we had a cocktail or two and talked about meaningless topics that came to the fore. Not sayin' I didn't smoke or drink some more. That would be testing the limits. But at some point I found myself asleep on the sofa usually reserved for me during these wanderings and began dreaming about food. Those are the best dreams. No backstabbing, no callbacks in the morning.

But in the wee hours guys like me get up and start looking for cheese and crackers or peanut butter and bread. Doesn't really matter all that much that I don't own these items. I'm hungry. Muncharinos! Food! Snacks! Whatever!

So it came to pass that in the year of our Lord, March 3rd, 2013, really early in the morning, I hit Flo's refrigerator with a passion not seen since Ryan O'Neal did the movie 'Love Story.' Don't remember much but I do know that I left a piece of steak with my teeth marks on it on the third shelf down in the refrigerary. Sure was good. Wasn't mine. Left my teeth marks in it.

Additionally, this morning, I left and absconded with a rolled entity that also did not belong to me. I have not wafted from this refectory as of yet. I shouldn't. It's not mine. But here it is. In the words of Tim O'Brien, "I have some thinkin' to do."

So, the point, if there is one, is that you should respect your friends and not do what I have done. Spend your life in sin and misery in the House of the Rising Sun. And keep your bicuspids out of your friend's meat. It ain't yours. Neither is the stuff on the table in the morning. Jeez, Flo, I'm a total shit!

Next day I'm down to the bridge and there still lies the note underneath the rock written by Eugene; "hey Jack, wanna buy a unicycle?" I'm busy with the toothpick getting the steak outta my teeth. Heard its getting warmer tomorrow.

SPRING BREAK

There I was in the middle of nowhere. It's a line I've used with women so many times. Never got me anywhere. This time was no exception.

In a little restaurant Flo and I sat at the bar and ordered some kind of Italian configuration. The waitress, all of six foot two and two hundred and sixty pounds yet with a disarming smile and beautiful blond hair said to us, "Whut kand I getcha?" This is the girl that Chum Lee from the pawn store TV show is looking for. Just for a few I wanted to be Chum Lee! Big ass bucking bronco!

Over to our left there was a couple. A gay guy and a gorgeous chick. I figured it all out immediately. The chick's boyfriend was at the boyfriend's, from the present bar experience, at a real one on one kinda situation. You try to re-write that sentence! Then our humungous glasses of wine showed up served by our humongous waitress with the nice blond hair. She was from Kentucky. Then I believe we ate some food. Served by the giant Amazon mentioned in some pre-Biblical texts. All I could think was that here, finally, is Chum Lee's girlfriend! She was nice.

Here, on the second week of college break, I found myself amidst a quarry. Why a quarry? It's the only word I could come up with. Nuts in paradise. I could probably say unkind words about kittens. Get me to the deck where I can write stuff!

I'm writing on Flo's deck. There aren't any kittens. Its quiet over here just outside of the hullabaloo. You sit here and think. I'm thinking. Thinking of the years I spent on a hillside in New York with, no doubt, the best personages a man can stick his can to, gentle, good people. People, pissed one moment, and best friends' the next. Your usual stuff. Can't find a situation better. Can't find better people. Last year...

Well, last year we all got the usual respect and helpfulness from a man down the hill, that gave us plumbing for our water truck. Nice guy. He's a whole other story. And one day I'm gonna write it! But, today, the big broad from Kentucky wants to flirt. She's the worst waitress I've ever seen. Big and bad. I want her now! The guy down the hill knows what I'm saying. Give me five minutes.

Anyways, I'm at Flo's, writing bullshit according to how it happened to me on this day. I had some Italian food and some salad. Drank some wine. Now, I'm off on a side street, away from the young party. It's a good place to be. The two of us, working on our computers, making the world safe from communism. Or the liberal left. Who needs the liberal left. Shouldn't we all have the right to anti-aircraft guns? But on Duval...

On Duval or somewhere nearby I met a Kentucky girl. She was full of life. Big as a statue. I bet she's thinking of me. I'm thinking of her. But, also, the beer is good. Think I'll sit here awhile and have a few. The company is good. The weather is fine. Got some thinkin' to do.

HOW MEN THINK

Firstly, I want to remark on the bartender's ass! EXEMPLARY! She doesn't care for me much but big whup!

I was at the Tiki Hut down the street hoping to run into Mila Kunis, who, rumor says, lives hereabouts. I just know that her and I will hit it off. And since I don't own any knives or guns its obvious that I'm trustworthy. Good-looking movie stars need to have trust in their neighbors. That's me. No guns. No knives!

Earlier in the day I was fishing down at Jack's Bridge. Per usual I didn't catch a Goddam thing. The tide is wrong. The wind is wrong. God in his benevolence is wrong! He's trying to show me a lesson. I stick my tongue out. Mila Kunis is taking a shower somewhere without me holding the soap and I can feel her loneliness. She is despondent over the lack of someone like me. As she should be. The sun circles the sky and I get caught up in other issues. They're not important. They're just 'other.'

My friend ,Johnny, the New York City Fireman, who squirmed and shuffled and dug for his buddies and cohorts those so many years ago, is back again. Haven't run into him yet but others have. I hope to have a few beers and shoot the shit and maybe play a little guitar with him. If I can keep the wolves at bay. The man was breathing glass that had cooked itself into a gas and settled into his lungs and given him a short life sentence. A good man. A hero. Yeah, I'll find him and toss back a few. People who need people are the luckiest people. In the world! The world is sometimes a very sad and sickening place.

Mila Kunis was said, by GQ Magazine, to be the sexiest woman in the world. Who am I to argue? And she just lives a few doors down. Somewhere. Check out her outfit in GQ. Did I mention my tomato plants? My tomato plants have much more clothing on than Mila Kunis in GQ Magazine. And that's all I have to say about that! I have fully clothed tomato plants in accordance to the dictates of the Catholic Church. And I'm a Southern Baptist! If everything goes better on a Ritz cracker then why not Mila? Just sayin'.

A day later some people came over and amongst them was Johnny and Mila. They were together and it seemed they were kind of interwoven. There was a Mila part here and a Johnny part there. I really couldn't tell which was which. I wasn't supposed to. Even though I fantasized every two minutes on this woman a true American hero had his arms about her. Jealousy, at this stage, was a dormant and dead thing. Heroes are supposed to get the chicks. Old worn out fisherman like me are not. It's the Karma. Bet Mila doesn't know its tarpon season. And that I'm the tarpon.

Young hot chicks don't know about fishing. The oneness between the castee and the caught. I can understand all that because we aren't all made in the image of the great fisher of men. Fisher of men? Does Jesus have a Key West address? What if he does? Mila looks a lot like Mary Magdalene, or so I'm told. The Catholics and Baptists tend to disagree on her countenance. Countenance is an old way of saying 'looks.' I'm not saying it. Religion is. Man it's hard to fish when you're thinking about sex objects! Maybe I should change the bait?

Then, out of the blue a couple is walking down my street enjoying the view and the beautiful houses and canals and palm trees and walks into my man cave. Its the one and only. She's with the other one and only. I don't panic. I offer them the same cheap ass beer I offer everyone. They accept. We talk about all kindsa bullshit and positivity and prosperity and stuff like that and even take a puff on a smoke. They're just good people. Before they leave she says, "You could hang three winter coats and two sweaters on that thing!"

Ain't got three winter coats. But I got twenty Hawaiian shirts with big smiles on their faces! Another day in paradise.

VOLUNTOWN

What I miss is going out of the driveway and heading toward Sterling. Almost immediately on Route 49 I come unto a dairy farm situated on both sides of the road. The spring flowers are showing off with no sense of humility, the cows are standing there stupidly looking one minute this way one minute off into space. Its maybe 78 degrees out with just an occasional cloud. There's bluegrass music on the college radio. Did I really have a chore to do or did I just want to drive through? My own personal drive through.

The property I own had an above ground pool in the front yard at one time. Pool is gone but the indentation and hole are not. I planted cherry, plum, pear and peach trees around the circle. In the middle a bit of tiger grass. Looks great. Birds crap there all the time.

Returning from this wonderful drive I'm still in ownership of this beautiful piece of land that I praise much more than any woman I've tried to woo. I get out of the car and the cats are doing roll over calisthenics in the grass. They're so damn happy! And of course the dead bird minus his head is lying next to the kitchen door. Better check the tomatoes.

In Key West, like Voluntown, I check my vegetable garden six or seven times a day. Its therapy. And I made it happen. It's the joy of having children. Did I overwater or underwater? Is the wind blowing hard enough to dry out the soil quickly? Will it rain any fucking time soon? Where's that prostitute I found on the internet? Just kidding. Thought the story was getting boring.

Outback I got the mancave. Big ass garage tent with much plenty room and another radio with same said college bluegrass radio station on. Its Peter Rowan time. I can live with it. One of the cats comes over and rubs against a leg after I've settled in a chair. There must be tons of things I could do to improve my status around here. They're all given consideration and promptly voted down in committee. The sarcasm wants to kick in but it's a beautiful day. Who the hell needs sarcasm? Look at those flowers pop! Every conceivable color in the universe is exploding like grenades made of artists' crayons. The cat jumps up and licks my face. A rabbit is eating weeds on the edge of the tall grass. A red tailed hawk floats overhead wondering if I am the enemy. What kind of developmental disorder do you have to have to put an above ground pool in the FRONT yard?

I'm not in Voluntown now. I'm in Key West. I've got something that acutely close to 100% of other people don't have. A spray bottle of IGUANA-RID. Like to say it works. Can't. The boys all got together right in front of me the other day and one of them said, "Hey where's the nut with the pancake syrup?" Pissed me off so I chased 'em away. Legs and tails flying everywhere.

Just as in New England there's 'deer crossing' signs on a lot of the islands. We have three. Deer. Not crossings. But when I go fishing the deer are never seen at the crossing sign. They seem to like to hang out by the sign that says, 'discharging of firearms prohibited in Monroe

County.' When I get up to the Everglades there's a 'panther crossing' sign. Just how much of our tax dollars was spent on teaching these guys to cross at the sign? Friggin' democrats!

Got a mancave here too. With a bunch of tomato plants off the ground so the aforementioned lizards don't get a free salad every night. Some red and green peppers. There's some basil and onions. Still practicing on this but the location closer to the equator causes great grief. A vegetable garden can burn up by the end of April around here no matter how much you tend it. There has to be some shade.

Haven't seen a mosquito in three months. The 4 inches of rain last night will take care of that. On the dock a great white heron has taken residence. He eats all the bait in the bait net half submerged in the canal. One time he stuck his beak into the netting and got stuck. Nearly flapped himself senseless as I found his blood-spattered body next day clinging to life by the thread of the net. Called the bird savior people and they took him away. Roommate got mad because I called them. How the hell would I know he spent the night in jail once for assaulting them? Why not assault an adult human male, get your ass kicked, and learn yer friggin' lesson?

In Voluntown in June life is a big baked cake with all the best icing. Some days are so action packed that I get to do my weekly dump run and come home with more than I took. Charlie Pride's 8-track tape of Golden Hits? Hell yeah! And on Saturday with a cold beer in hand its 'Prairie Home Companion' with all your favorite Guy Noir stuff and Rusty the cowpoke. And the cats. And some beer. Summer. And the livin' is easy.

THE DEAD GUY

Don Juan Esperanza, known as, well, Don, was fishing out on the Gulf side mangroves in shallow water.

He was in a twenty-foot skiff used mostly in shallow waters for the purpose of catching blackfish and sometimes tarpon. Today, specifically, he was fishing for red snapper in a place where they were otherwise unknown. Its not often you catch on a rumor and get to act on it. Today Don was Action Jackson.

Things started slow enough. Only thing biting were mosquitos and indeterminate botherings of whatever kind. Everyday isn't the best fishing day. Sometimes fishing is like a bout of the flu. You're just sick. But in the peculiar and particular events of this day fish were going to weave their wonderful magic.

After five minutes of anchorage the three rods were all pulling with fish. Two had bait, one had a lure. It was a deep-set pleasure that came to Don's mind that luck had finally caught up with him. He pulled in line over line of red snapper, grouper, and yellow tail. The back of the boat began to fill with the legal maximum catch of each one. When he reached that goal he purposefully tossed back the overlimits and went after the mangrove snapper. These were no babies. Every fish was in excess of five pounds. It was Easter Sunday and God looked down in all his benevolence. "Look at the Goddam fish!"

There were some manatees swimming by and their human-ness was something that always took you aback. They were bodies of the mammal sort and kindred to every other mammal. Didn't take to hooks and bait though. Usually travelled in ones and twos. Seemed to be three. Don didn't really care as there were fish biting from all points of the compass rose. Every catch was a few more pounds than the previous. Currently the heaviest was on the line with a lure. Not much fight but big! Don took to reeling it in fighting with the rig and spool and tiring over the weight. Big motherhunker! And there it was, on the side of the gunwale, a hundred and eighty pound Anglo Saxon. Human! "Gotta be shittin' me!"

There was no doubt as to the lifelessness of the man on the end of the line. He was dead. Smackers. Don sat and took a deep swig of the cold beer. Then he opened the cooler and took out a bottle of Southern Comfort. Multiple shots. What to do. The other two lines were pulling, pulling like they had never done before in his whole post Mariel Boatlift life. Another shot. Then he began to bring in the lines and, alas, to cast them again. Every line brought a fish. There was a dead man floating next to the boat. The sun shone beautifully like ripe corn in the sky. Ripe corn and a dead guy.

Don pulled the dead guy into the boat. He wanted to check his wallet to see on who he was. He couldn't get into a robbery motive. The eyes were closed and that was a relief. This wasn't Don's first dead guy. Dead people show up on the shores and waterways of the keys everyday. There's Haitian, Cuban and South American bodies washing up like bad habits. Add to that the snorkeling, skin diving and careless tourists who don't have a clue. Open eyes were the worst. The fish and crabs had long ago gotten to them. But without a radio or a cell phone, because a cell phone would deteriorate out here in this salt and was better left in the car, there was no way to contact any official entity. Look at those fishing lines bent double!

After careful consideration and a rope around the waist of the dead guy, who being already dead, was hefted over the side and the fishing continued. Why not? The fishing was good. The lines were like arches over the Delaware Bay Bridge! Great weights were on the fishing lines.

Sharks! Sharks are no big danger in the keys. Usually a variety that creates a nuisance by announcing that they know you're catching fish and they want their share. Not always. There's a few Great Whites about and bull sharks. But usually just harmless sharks that like to strip your catch right off the line because of their opportunistic personalities. Or pay attention to the dead guy tied to the starboard side. The dead guy was missing an arm and a leg in no time. Don was aghast and alarmed and friggin' out of his mind. He thought he might fish for a while longer and eventually head in and turn the dead guy in to the Coast Guard or County Sheriff. Now between them there was only a man and a half and one of them was dead. Doubled over line brought in a mutton snapper. "Jesus, this ain't fair." Suddenly the dead man was totally gone. There was nothing tied to the boat and no indication that there ever had been.

Don was at his personal crossroads. His Catholicism and the legal code he had learned under Castro's Cuba all told him what he must do. All the learnings from his mother and his father directed him to the righteous path. His aunts and uncles were there along with the Virgin Mary. His way was clear. There was no choice.

Don continued fishing. He moved his boat about a mile to alleviate the sharks and he continued on his record setting catch. It was too bad about the dead guy but there were a half a dozen dead guys found floating in the keys every day. There had never been a fishing day like this. The yellowtail and mutton kept coming. Species not well-known literally jumped in the boat but all were fat, edible and salable. All three poles bent with beckoning fish. Guilt meshed with a purity of fun and the last pole on the last cast of the night brought excitement not yet experienced. The last catch was probably a monster grouper and a big moneymaker down at the fish store. One hell of a day!

The reel tightened and grew taut. The fight was on between the two adversaries. It was perhaps forty five minutes later that Don, having thought badly of himself and his guilt toward the Catholic Church, and having had countless moments of self-doubt and trepidation, and now quite hungry after a day of fishing and winning the lottery in the fish catching business, brought to the boat a wide eyed, absolutely stunningly resemblant of the first dead guy.

"You gotta be shittin' me!"

A WORD IN EDGEWISE

In my summer travels throughout New England and New York I get to spend time with people so immersed with good memories that I'm led to imagine an old saddle horse. Trustworthy, easy to be around, good company and knows where it's going.

Other times when drawn into easygoing conversation there's a person who takes the verbal lead and never thinks of relinquishing it. They've done this the most and the fastest. They've been to every event and met the most important people. They drink only top of the line beer made by a brewery that the rest of us have no access to and bathe with soap endorsed by Beyoncé and Madonna. Everything they have done or accomplished is fodder for a one-way conversation. If you do get a word in edgewise your topic is checkmated because the other party did it better. If there's a group in this conversation it's hardly ever noticed by the primary speaker that I have slipped the bonds of excessive verbiage and self-flagellation. At these times saying nothing and hearing nothing approaches Godliness. Take a walk and see how the campgrounds are coming along. Take along a cheap beer available to any and everyone and revel in the cleanness of the dollar shampoo smell that follows me everywhere.

So it took me by surprise that I would be sitting on a barstool at the Parrot listening to some Gossipy Gus telling me his poor history with women. Since it wasn't something I wanted to discuss I listened in a half assed manner knowing the escape hatch to Whitehead Street was just behind me.

"I'm tellin' ya I made some mistakes when I dissed or discarded the average looking chick, or the chick with a few extra pounds. These women adored the ground I walked on. They fed me, bought me liquor, would submit to any sexual act this side of bestiality and cleaned my house. I accepted their kindnesses and, I guess, abused them in the sense that I showed no emotion towards them. If I demanded they undress they would be naked before me in no time." He ordered an expensive beer from a brewery in East Podunk, Pennsylvania. Then right back to his mindless story.

"Now you take your good looking chick, the beautiful woman with adoring hordes following her around and somehow you score. She's your girlfriend and you spend the night at each other's homes. You make dinners together and share glasses of wine. Your chest expands when people check her out when you shop together at the grocery store. You are one lucky man."

"Then she starts in with crap like 'why don't we go to this party' or 'lets visit my old friends.' You just know that she wants to show you off to her old boyfriend whose always gonna be present at these convenient soirees. And somewhere along the line you break up for a while then get back together. When you do get back together she wants to go to parties again and show you off or just make someone plain jealous."

I made to interject while ordering another cheap beer. "It's been my exp..."

"No, no man, you ain't listening. You take my advice based on my experience and you'll go a long way. People know me from all over the country and if one said I was a genius with women then a hundred did. And I guess I am. Not many people have had the luck of the pursuit as I have. But, I'll tell ya, them semi-ugly ones with a few pounds packed on will do anything, ANYTHING I tell ya." He got up to pee.

Why I didn't leave is beyond me or at least change my seat. The bouncers called 'dance instructors' at the Parrot were chatting it up with the tourists in this relatively peaceful scene. The verbal guy returned.

"I'll tell ya this bar ain't got nothing on Benny's in St. Louis. That joint is rockin'! My good friend the lead guitar player in Smash has a bar in Boston that makes this place look like a mortuary. This bank president I know has a restaurant that caters to all the movie stars that have been nominated for Academy Awards." Ad infinitum...

I clocked him. Broke his nose. Before the blood had even dripped onto his exclusively made Hawaiian shirt the dance instructors had me out on the sidewalk. They all knew me and told me to take off quick, maybe come back next week. This I did. I walked rapidly past the sign that said, 'Hemingway Pissed Here' and onto the side streets where my pace slowed. I enjoyed the walk and the most I said the rest of the day was a few hellos and a thank you or two.

WILLARD, HENRY S GRANDSON

I was quite taken aback one day recently when a Key West rooster approached me and said, "hey mang. How you roll?"

He was dressed in the style of shorts that are cut below the shin, made of denim, and hanging totally below his ass and held up only by some Caribbean witchdoctor hoodoo. He made some kind of hand sign that distorted his fingers and could only have been notice that he was in a gang of some kind. A chicken in a gang in Old Town Key West. In actuality not even close to the everyday weirdness of the place.

"I be Henry's grandson and I 'member when you come over da house. You good for a white dude." First thing that came to mind was that he wasn't black and he had to be well aware of that fact. He was a chicken. A kind of red and brown rooster. Then it hit me who he was. My old friend from way back from 'Nam to this here rock. This was the grandson of my old friend Henry. That was the Henry run over by a tourist while trying to decide whether to go to a sex club or go out and eat fried conch. The maintenance man from the hotel across the street from Flo's house and a local Bahamian woman had played badminton with his corpse via a chain link fence for several days. This was Willard, the grandson.

Willard had been a problem to his parents since the day he was hatched. He was always in trouble with the law in some form or other and was a strain on the county juvenile justice system. He stole cars, purses, cocktails, basically anything without a person paying attention. His favorite theft was the three-wheeled pedi-cab. One of those guys stopped for a coffee or a soda or a hit on a pipe and Willard was off down Caroline Street with the wind in his beak. Sold them for scrap to a local Cuban crime boss. "Ah, Willard, you're the spitting image of your grandpa."

Actually that wasn't true. He had had someone twist his feathers near his head into a Rastafarian braid that a lot of kids have to prove that they are righteous potheads. I garnered that he needed a bath. It just sort of went with the braids. Unnoticed until this moment I also surmised his Malcolm X tee shirt, a little dirty, that came down right above his pants. Presumably this was so that you got to get the full benefit of seeing his pants below his ass. Unlike his grandpa he had no originality. I asked what he had been doing the last several years since his grandfather's passing.

"I be goin' ta college one day a week studyin' fish an water and stuff like dat. I work out de sex club on Duval passin' out de flyers. Keeps me in grass." I wanted to know more because I was an old friend of the family. The bonds between his grandfather and me were rock solid. He told me more as I questioned and was answered and I sort of got a biography. It was interesting enough.

Willard got in trouble in his early teens to the degree that he became the only chicken ever allowed into the Florida Sheriffs' Association Boy's Town upstate. After he got out he bummed around in the Everglades for a while, just like his 'pawpaw,' and learned how to thatch Tiki hut roofs from the Seminoles. It was a good living but he soon tired of catfish and alligator steak in his daily regimen and headed back home to Bahama Village. He hung out at the Circle K on Duval and got to know every degenerate, crook, drunk and tranny in the keys. He went to rehab twice but just couldn't quit the ganja. He got a hen pregnant but the cats ate all his chicks so he gave up on having children. His mother and father were icons in the community but they didn't want him around what with the braids and the marijuana smell following him around everywhere. His mother, a Bryn Mawr graduate, just couldn't stomach his pants around his knees. "Why in the world, child, do you have your boxers up to your navel and your pants around your knees?" He always had an answer. Just didn't make sense.

"You seein' ma and pa?" he asked. I told him I thought so and we parted ways after a few more words that I didn't always understand. It was a sunny day like most others. The bougainvillea were quite in bloom but as yet no frangipani. I thought I would indeed go see Fred and Clara. I enjoyed my walk amongst the tourists reveling in the sun and the Conch Trains passing me on the street.

On Olivia Street I stopped at a well-manicured fenced yard and gradually sauntered up past the gate and onto the porch. Between the knock and my departing Fred and Clara and I had a most wonderful hour or so of looking back and sometimes forward. Clara poured gin and tonics and history poured from our lips. Fred had been a doctor for many many years. He was by far the most educated chicken on the island. He had rows and rows of books on his shelves and most related to higher literature of the sort where Nobels and Pulitzers were awarded. He had every book by Dreiser, Balzac, Hemingway and Faulkner. I spent some time perusing. Always liked literate people and I felt at home here. In my mind chickens were people too. Knowing that I had other things to do and look at I took my leave after a brief reminisce of their son Henry. We all shed a silent tear.

Back out on the street I wandered aimlessly just watching people and events. There sure were a lot of people on cell phones and Blackberries and not watching where they were going. There were drunk college girls and puking college boys who had tried to inhale the smoke of a Cuban cigar. There were bikers and weightlifters and cross dressers and moms and dads. There were cross-dressing moms and dads!

I heard a siren in the distance but it meant nothing. I heard a noise from behind me that sounded like people screaming and swearing. It appeared a few people were chasing something but it was all a long way off. Suddenly, out of the literate blue, there was a chicken, hair all braided up, pants down to his nether regions and puffing on a long joint the size of an athletic sock, came Willard cranking his legs like crazy with a wild look in his eye on a pedi-cab. He turned on two wheels down Caroline and was gone!

I sure loved that family.

A TERRORIST IN PARADISE

Delbert McClinton Mohammad was a jihadist.

At this very moment traveling on a Greyhound bus out of Miami headed to the Keys. His plan was to blow up Naval Air Station Key West or, at least, as many fighter jets as he could attack before being taken down and receiving his promised virgins. But he liked the scenery. It was a bright sunshiny Florida day through Islamorada and the Seven Mile Bridge. Del, as he wished to be called, had earlier decided that he would do a little vacationing on this side of heaven's gate before he gave his life for the cause. Virgins were fine but he'd like to deal with the 'experienced' type of woman before he had to do all that de-flowering. Plenty of time. He wasn't given a deadline, so to speak.

In Key West he took a pedi-cab to a bed and breakfast and checked in. He got to his room and unpacked his clothes, his bits of snacks and the c-4 explosive and timer. He'd buy a gun later at a local store and because it was Florida didn't anticipate any problems. He was an American. He'd become a Mohammad much later. On the agenda were cocktails, maybe a little ganja, and definitely some women who seemed plentiful to his casual eye. Wasn't but twenty short minutes before he hit the Green Parrot and started downing cheap beer. It was just past four on an Autumn afternoon and the sky was still full of sun. Tourist women abounded. Del wandered off in his mind to a nice eye-watering buzz.

Joe Beans had his buzz on also but as yet could still fathom the needs of his mission. He needed some wild drugs or money to purchase same. If he took his meds as prescribed by the Veterans Administration he would be sane as a president but he didn't and sold his legal drugs for vodka and went to play polo in his head. That game was on hold as he was in a bedroom at a bed and breakfast and was rifling through someone's belongings looking for cash. Not quite sober as a president but yet not totally wasted Joe Beans knew c-4 explosive when he saw it. He had spent a year in the Ia Drang Valley in Viet Nam. C-4 was common as Hershey bars. In some ways, he thought, better than cash! Joe Beans went out to meet his night. It seems hardly possible that c-4 explosive could be in deadlier hands than a jihadist. But it was.

Harry Denks was the unluckiest professional fisherman in the Keys. And his inheritance money was running low. He trailered his 28-foot fiberglass fishboat with twin 300 horsepower Yamaha engines all over the islands. His gig was that he'd bring the charter to you. He made good money, over a thousand bucks a day sometimes, but no one ever caught fish of any consequence. That reputation catches up with you.

Harry would take off in his car sometimes and visit the Tiki Hut on Sugarloaf. There were always a bunch of semi-friendly semi-locals to shoot the shit with. And with no charter on a particular day he saw no reason not to while it away sipping cold beers and the occasional gin and tonic. He toked on his cigarette and dreamed of better days or maybe a hot woman walking into the bar. The other charter captains were reaping record rewards!

Later in the evening Del found himself on the 800 block on Duval Street. He had met several lovely women and was sure there were going to be several more. But at present he was in a low-lighted booth in a bar with a striking redhead who had her hands down his pants. That she was gorgeous was obvious to anyone and Del was breaking champagne bottles in his mind as he launched the USS Mohammad! Red sky at night, a sailor's delight.

Joe Beans, by now extremely inebriated and staggering around Higgs Beach, had lost his intentions. He had a plan to sell something but he just couldn't quite remember what it was. He took another chug of rotgut vodka and puked on his threadbare sneakers. This was noticed by an old female friend of his who had similar mental defects. It wasn't long before she had him in the bushes making him sexual promises while consuming his booze. After he passed out she removed the block of c-4 from his pocket. She had no idea what it was and so when she got up from the crabgrassed ground and walked to her next destiny she tossed the block into a boat sitting on a trailer with twin 300-horsepower Yamahas.

There must be a voice in some people's minds that says something like, "You've gone too far!" That would be some people but not in people who exist on this planet like Del. Del had decided that his exploratory surgery using both hands was needed on this particular occasion and proceeded toward that exact event. Well, expecting a coke and getting a root beer might be depressing but expecting what he was expecting and finding a penis was a different story altogether. Still, with the alcohol and all, it took several minutes for the confirmation. He took the exit, stage left. And upchuck he did.

The next day Harry Denks got a last minute charter. Some rich dude from Wall Street renting a house at $5000 a week. He wanted a half-day so Harry took him out past American Shoals and chummed for yellow tuna. As all days just as gorgeous as a newborn baby, the water calm, the heat not unbearable. Then for hours and hours despite moving the boat around nothing happened. Nothing happened at all. Not even an albatross! Harry's reputation seemed to be sealed by an act of great Neptune. Frankly Harry was beginning to see himself as a general loser. No argument here.

Joe Beans was awake and coherent. This was unusual. Sometimes a transformation would happen without his prescriptions. This was the day. And a fairly large block of stolen c-4 was missing! And he wanted to give Cathy a slap and get his rotgut vodka back. He went for the explosives first. Hell, it was the right thing to do.

Del was kind of out of it for a while. He could walk but not so well. His mission to destroy Naval Air Station Key West came to mind. He was in trouble with the mullah. And apparently he had sinned. In several ways. If we gave Del a pony and gave him a TV series maybe that would have changed his outlook. But no. Delbert McClinton Mohammad was a jihadist of the first degree. That he liked to play dice with the trannys in those darkened bars was another story altogether. Sorry, Islam, this guy ain't a good candidate!

Harry had a client for fishing on Lower Sugarloaf at the Bait Shop. The guy was a movie producer doing some location scouting and wanted to do some fishing out on American Shoals. They stocked up on bait and beer and took off for the deep water. Drifting with the tide they caught a few small yellowtail but nothing of any significance. The producer was getting irked because all he heard every day on the radio at dinnertime was how much fish the other charters were catching. Harry's results were quite unsatisfactory. If only they knew that a swarm of bluefin tuna were feeding below only a few yards distant. Purely out of boredom Harry started cleaning his boat of things that were biodegradable. Among the items he threw overboard was an odd clay like cake he had never seen before.

Some things about c-4 are not known. Specifically what water and water pressure might do to it. About a minute after the cake sank into the water there was a huge explosion about 50 feet down. It shocked them both and the producer spilled his beer all over himself. In a few seconds dead and live tuna were swarming the boat near the surface. With eyes agog the two fishermen studied the situation not knowing just what had blown up or why. But fish are fish and they proceeded to harvest the dead ones just as their lines grew taut.

When he answered his cell phone Dell was confronted with the voice of his mullah. The boss jihadist screamed and cajoled with the worker bee jihadist. Dell had a hangover and was feeling quite guilty about diddling a tranny in that dark, dank bar. He regretted not waiting on his virgins. The gist and finality of that conversation was that Dell had better get his ass over to the Naval Air Station and start doing some damage. And Dell and his hangover proceeded to do just that. But first he ripped open the 8 ball of cocaine he had purchased from the tranny and started snorting lines. God was great!

Forgetting what he was doing was a Joe Beans specialty. So he forgot about the c-4 and went looking for liquor. He found one of his hobo buddies down on Higgs Beach and lifted his half empty bottle of vodka. Life was grand. Then he forgot some more. After a while he forgot everything.

At the gate of NAS Key West there was a young recruit just issued his first M-1 with live ammunition and a sidearm. He served in the Coast Guard on shore duty. He was lovingly and endearingly referred to as 'the idiot.'

When Harry and the producer got back to Sugarloaf they counted seventeen tuna weighing anywhere from 50 to 150 pounds. They decided to sell most of the catch to the A&B Lobster House just off Duval for big cash and of course kept a few for themselves and friends. The producer expressed quite vehemently that he would tell all his friends about Harry's fishing acumen. The explosion, although not understood was quickly forgotten and Harry would become a big name in the charter fishing industry. The producer made a movie about the underside of life in Key West and gave Harry a bit part. He played a dress salesman who sold exclusively to cross dressers and the like but got his name in the credits. It was a flop everywhere but in the Keys and Provincetown, Massachusetts.

Del, not the smartest jihadist, drove into the gate of NAS Key West in a broken down Toyota with great-looking mag wheels he had purchased off a Puerto Rican kid on Stock Island. 'The idiot' waved him down but the mission for Allah was so important that Del did not stop. What he was going to do without his c-4 and only a .20 caliber pistol with just two bullets is anybody's guess. But there was no need for guessing as 'the idiot,' from a family related to the Hatfields of West Virginia and an excellent shot holed all four tires with just four shots. The other MPs quickly surrounded the car and arrested the worst jihadist since the guy who tried to blow up his shoes on an airliner some years back. 'The idiot' was promoted and awarded a silver star. He wears 'idiot' as a badge of honor to this day. Del is on a hunger strike in Guantanamo. He never tells his brothers about the tranny on Duval Street.

Joe Beans sobers up once in a while and meets friends at the Green Parrot for beers. He shouldn't drink at all but when he takes his meds he's sober as a judge. Or a president. And he's always clean-shaven and wearing clean clothes. During these times he thinks back to an event where he was sure he stole some c-4. But he just can't be sure. Probably never happened at all.

DIRK DINGLE

Rik Matson walked along the street in a place called paradise smelling the cooking aromas from the various kitchens, watching the girls playing on their smart phones, and generally feeling completely at ease. He hadn't had a vacation in years and this place with its palm trees and laid-back ambiance was just the ticket for forgetting the recent past.

He stopped in a few places and had a few beers while striking up conversations with the barmaids and whomever seemed in a friendly mood. That a few people stared at him for a moment or two and nudged their drinking partners didn't affect him in the smallest degree. The sunshine was a constant and his demeanor could not be diverted into any sort of negativism. Along a small back alley he stopped in a small restaurant ordering a porterhouse steak with a green tossed salad with avocado and a glass of Guinness. His waitress paused for a moment wondering if by any chance he might be some famous guy from television or the newspapers. Rik was quite used to this treatment and let it slide like a shadowy boa constrictor onto the floor and out the exit.

Later he made inquiries down at the docks for a fishing charter expedition the next day. He knew there were still tarpon out there and quite a bit of yellowtail. The tuna had been gone for over two months but that was the luck of the draw. He had dreamed of a fishing excursion for several years now and he had been told by co-workers of the weird and salacious environment of the Florida keys. He wasn't looking for any physical excitement other than the luring and retrieving of large living fish. He remembered, as a kid, his dad taking him out in boats in the gulf from his hometown of Biloxi, Mississippi. Those were happy times and after every trip he and his father would clean the fish and take them home to his mom who would make hush puppies and fry the fish in onions and green peppers and serve them with crispy French fries. That was before dementia took his dad and a hit and run driver took his mom who had just run out for beer to serve with one of the fish dinners. The charter boat trip salesman gave him a look of familiarity and stared just a little too long. Rik took his ticket and receipt and returned to his hotel room.

After the demise of his family when Rik was 18 years old he found himself penniless and without the comfort of a college education. This, of course, had changed over the ensuing years. He had found a career and performed quite admirably and was paid more than handsomely for his efforts. He was beyond wealthy compared to the average wage earner. He didn't own a computer endeavor nor was he the owner of a vast empire of any sort. He had some stocks and bonds. He had several parcels of property in Connecticut and Mississippi and kept turning down high-end offers for their purchase. He always kept eight hundred dollars in his pocket and several thousand dollars in travelers' cheques in his luggage. He didn't wear jewelry though, not even a watch, and usually dressed in off the rack clothes or even items he found in thrift stores. He sold stock when advised to and always turned a neat profit. And now he found that he would never have to work again if he so chose.

After his nap in the hotel room Rik headed out into Duval and Caroline Streets for a little adventure. In a biker and tattoo bar he met a girl named Nancy and they struck an immediate chord. This was such a nice thing for Rik as his relationships over the past ten years had been fleeting. Nancy was darkly tanned with deep brown hair with sun-bleached ends that enhanced a beautiful and contagious smile. She also thought he was familiar but he was so nice and soothing and comforting in his countenance that she was drawn to his personal aura. They talked of many things big and small concerning family, the world, the daily news and her pet kittens. The barmaid serving drinks gave him long looks and hovered nearby with always a crossways glance. The night grew long and they hit several more bars, never drinking too much or too fast. Rik invited Nancy on his fishing trip and she quickly acquiesced. They took their leave of each other deep into the night and were to meet the day after tomorrow. They kissed long and slowly at the entrance to her rooms on Margaret Street and departed somewhat enthralled with each other.

There was a reason people kept glancing at Rik and wondering who he might be. After his mother's death Rik travelled to California looking for work and adventure. He found adventure but very little work other than as barback or dishwasher and that ilk. He once got rolled in a dive bar in San Diego and lost the last hundred bucks to his name. That didn't go over well with the supervisor of the rooming house who gave him three days to get 'sufficient' employment. Rik answered an advertisement to a casting call for extras in a soon to be made movie about relationships in southern California. The relationships actually meant porno and Rik did not know what to do. But the $150 daily to just hang around naked did the trick, as it were, and that's how it all started. At first a hundred fifty daily and then $30,000 per film for about forty hours work. It wasn't always easy as the producer and director wanted action in the stimulation of his male member. That can't always happen as every male has his drooping point. The producer, an ace in this market, already knew of this malady and served up females on the sidelines to entice his body parts to do what they wanted. Then he walked back out on the set and did as asked.

After several years Rik was becoming a big star, so to speak, and the producers and directors got together and gave him a name. It was Dirk Dingle! And there was a reason for that particular name. His parents left him no discernible endowments except one; a fishing pole to die for! After obtaining a lawyer and an agent Rik's income per movie went up to close to $500,000 per movie and he could make as many as five per month. He was young, well hung and had no relatives to exact shame on to. He became so famous that sex stores across the country couldn't keep his videos and DVD's in stock.

But money isn't everything. Rik wasn't real happy with himself. He knew that all of his friends from high school probably were all caught up in his fame. His minister down at the Baptist church was probably having sleepless nights. In bedrooms all over the country the male would exclaim, "hey, I'm Dirk Dingle!" It was time to get out, and again, so to speak. Rik quit the industry, moved to Montana, and one day decided to go to Key West. He started using his real name and dyed his hair several different colors over time. He always wore loose fitting slacks. That part of his life was done.

Nancy was divorced and happily without children. She wasn't looking for a mate or to even 'meet up.' Her life had all the foibles that led a woman to move to paradise to just exist and work on her tan. Rik was a charmer and quite good-looking but damn if he didn't look familiar. She pulled out a DVD and put it into the player. It was titled, "Dirk Does Detroit." Can't beat that for kismet!

But this isn't a pornographic story. It's a very odd love story. Rik and Nancy went fishing on the charter. She never told him what she knew but was aware that all the other fishermen and women kept giving them sidelong glances. The fishing was very good. The kingfish were running and biting hard and putting up great fights. After a while Rik started overhearing remarks concerning Dirk Dingle. He was very happy when the boat started heading for the docks where he and Nancy vacated themselves immediately after selling their fish to the first mate. Once again Rik's monetary acumen not only saved but made him money. They went to his room, showered, did not make love and headed off to the Green Parrot. Where they met a drunk. Not a regular drunk but a loudmouthed over the top verbal alcoholic who, as luck would have it, was a collector of pornography. "Hey, its Dirk Dingle!"

Unfortunately, Joe Beans was there on a bender and he definitely knew who Dirk Dingle was. So did over 70 percent of the female customers and that led to bedlam, blasphemy and bartending misconstructions! Nancy told him that she already knew his story and that, of course, loosened him up and he began signing autographs for the adoring and sometimes jealous fans. The drunk pornography collector got louder and louder and tried to act as agent to this misplaced movie actor and his new found girlfriend. That was remedied when Joe Beans kneed him in the groin. Rik bought Joe a couple of drinks and a couple of shots on top of that and pretty soon Joe Beans was out on the street staggering around. Such was his way in the world.

Rik adjusted to the fame that he did not endeavor for and nightly signed photographs, sometimes breasts, and a few thighs. His celebrity was mostly light hearted and usually low key. Nancy didn't mind and encouraged him to keep a cool head. So to speak. They grew deeply in love and married. After a year in an Old Town two bedroom they bought a house on Lower Sugarloaf, obtained a fishing boat, spending tons of time on the American Shoals jigging for tuna. They never had children but seemed quite happy with each other and on Saturdays they would invite friends over to listen to Prairie Home Companion on the radio while serving mojitos on the patio or in the mancave. They grew older together in happiness. Everyone knew his background but not one soul gave a single shit and time moved on. Just last week Rik bought a larger boat and named it the Miss Nancy. Everyone on the island calls it 'The Dingle.'

Not every story has an intricate plot. Sometimes it's just a good little story. If you'll excuse me Rik has just made me a new mojito. Life ain't so bad if you just let it play itself out.

JOE FINDS JESUS

Hay Soos von Klampt was and is a hippie of the sort you used to see thirty years ago. More like 40 years ago. Called himself Jesus. Go figure.

Found himself on the archipelago pinching drinks and hanging out with weirdos. Didn't care. Daddy left a trust fund. For all intents and purposes he was Jesus with a credit card. The sun came up. The sun went down.

Joe Beans, not quite drunk to his regular degree, fell into the Parrot, in his way, and ordered a draft beer. None of the popcorn-eating clientele seemed to bother to notice. It was a Joe Beans night. Three quarters moon, thirty bucks in his pocket.

The first thing Joe Beans noticed was that there was a guy in a long ass skirt with brown shoulder length hair drinking beer at the bar. Damned if he didn't look like Jesus (Gee-sus). If you're half on your ass on cheap domestic beer and you see a guy what looks like your savior then you might have something to say. Joe Beans did. And he did.

"Hey, Mr. Jesus, are you my savior and protector? Yeah you, I'm talkin' to you!"

Well, Jesus turned around, not knowing he was the acting savior and said, "Can I help you?" From that moment on the biggest bar fight ensued ever known to the Lower Keys. A well-known drunk and Jesus went at it for about twenty minutes. Not once was scripture ever mentioned. No one mentioned Mary. There certainly were a lot of 'motherfucks!'

I watched outside as the devil fought Jesus to a standstill over a period of about twenty minutes. The dance instructors just stood back and let the action play itself out. It was a mess.

I picked Joe up at the county jail next day having been released on his own recognizance, known and dearly loved by all the sheriff's deputies. We got a six-pack at the Circle K and drank it at a parking lot on Smathers Beach. I asked Joe why he beat the guy up.

"Got trouble with religion."

"What's religion got to do with anything?"

"You saw who he looked like."

"Looked like a hippie."

"Looked like Jesus," said Joe.

"Calls himself that too," I said.

"No shit, back from the dead. Again." Joe took off toward Higgs Beach no doubt to rummage around in his bag of stuff under his favorite bush while the gerbils ran the little wheel inside his head.

I ran into Mr. von Klampt several more times during his stay in paradise. He was always in the company of one or two gorgeous women or college girls. The girls seemed entranced with him and he had an eerie Charles Manson-like hold on them. At least that's what I told my single, devoid of any sexual prospects self. He did look like the ubiquitous household portrait I've seen in the homes of the pseudo religious. He would even sometimes speak in a manner that seemed to mimic Biblical verse. But usually his topic of the moment or any moment for that matter was 'pussy.' I didn't speak with him much but I usually sat or stood close enough by to get an earful about his last conquest, his next and the manner in which he partook. The man was a slob, as crass as they come, and still endowed with an aura that at least some strikingly attractive ladies found fascinating. I thought to myself that too bad, in this town, he wasn't gay and I could write about him making fishers of men.

Jesus always paid with his credit card and left a hefty tip. He was even let back into the Parrot although he had been a participant in a bar brawl. He was appreciated for his tipping charity but everyone soon tired of his one-subject topic. He was medicinal to me in one aspect. Upon hearing him preach his dissertations on conquests and such I found I no longer aspired as much to search out that entity myself. He reduced a woman and fellow human being to a lusty restaurant dish. I started paying way more attention to what a woman had to say rather than staring at her boobs or wondering what my chances were. In fact Jesus made me want to go fishing. For fish!

Out on the bridge before noon on a Monday the sun caressed my bare chest and face. There was a cloud or two on the horizon but nothing threatening. I was fishing but rarely caught anything but it didn't matter. It was my Zen time. There were no obstructions or cranial roadblocks to my happiness here. The Navy fighter jets took off from Boca Chica for their practice runs out beyond Tortugas. They made me feel safe. The solitary spot that put me in a state of grace and made me feel as one with the world or maybe even my lord in those times when I was believing. It was a damn good thing that the fake Jesus didn't know about this spot for that would have wrecked the whole deal and despoiled my correspondence with my maker.

Kismet, chance and coincidence fills my life. And so it was that I was in the Smoking Tuna listening to a country band sing off color songs. Joe Beans in his sober suit of shorts, clean t-shirt and flip flops showed up to heft a few with me. He hadn't been drinking that rot gut vodka that puts him in a delusional state so we were able to converse, observe our surroundings and enjoy each other's company. The band played a song that an old buddy from up north used to sing at open mikes and talent nights. It was called, "She Left Me for Jesus." It was about a white redneck losing his girlfriend to a Mexican named Haysoos. Of course the redneck in question called him Jesus and so the song went on. It was funny. Until Jesus actually showed up with his adoring entourage.

Drunk or sober Joe Beans didn't care one whit for Jesus. And so Jesus got bloodied again. As did Joe, myself and a few other customers. The band played silly obnoxious songs like they were in a Texas roadhouse and laughed their asses off. The good-looking disciples of Jesus scrummed up close together and yelped a lot. This guy really did have Charles Manson written all over him.

At some point someone called the cops and who shows up but the Police Chief himself, an openly gay yet kind and intelligent man who was also friends with Joe Beans. The chief and some of his minions broke up the fight at which point Jesus made a reference to the chief's sexual orientation in a detrimental manner. Joe Beans didn't need to expend any more savagery upon the chosen one as the chief took his turn and showed what an ex-member of

Special Forces can do with his hands. Wasn't pretty. After a night in the slammer the chief put Jesus on a Greyhound bound for Miami with his own personal funds and said, "don't come back!" He left without his pussy.

Joe Beans and I went down to the Bottle Cap and while we were partaking of our first beers some of the disciples showed up and started a conversation with us. They certainly were gorgeous and pretty well educated too. Turned out to be DEA agents with time on their hands. Joe and I had a blast but we were very respectful and as such were served a pleasing bounty. I never saw Jesus again. Amen.

TAKING A WRONG TURN

It was a drug run. We were to meet our contact, "Vinny," somewhere out near American Shoals. Captain Maurice had his eyes peeled for the go-fast boat supposedly coming from the southwest. Little did he know that soon he would be nesting, like so many spoonbills, in his own little rookery atop a mangrove island.

Sometimes during the day unmarked C-130s would fly over very low either to check us out or to mar satellite photos concerning their own quasi-legal missions in Central America. We were on different sides of the same business yet both on the wrong side of the law. There were other fishing boats around too. It was very likely that some of the other boats were doing exactly what we were doing. What we were doing was trying to make a whole lot of money very fast!

I met Mo down at the Parrot while sipping a few beers with my last few dollars. We had chatted before but nothing of consequence. It occurred to me that he was throwing out hints regarding reaping some square grouper, the name locals used to describe a marijuana bale. I didn't care to do any law breaking but there damn sure wouldn't be many more beers in my future with the existent empty pockets.

"Jack, you can make a fortune!"

"I'll do it."

That's all it took and over the next few days we moved his 18-foot underpowered fishing skiff to different docks to create plausible alibis if we were discovered after the fact. If we were discovered during the fact there was only one outcome. We were fucked! Mo told me the day and time we were to depart and so I went home to wait. I pulled out some Hemingway as it seemed appropriate and spent several days in my hammock reading and napping.

On our departure day I awoke a little befuddled and pulled on the same shorts I wore yesterday. I got the coffee maker going and turned on channel seven because all the talking heads were 25-year-old women dressed in soft porn outfits. The weather girl in her body tape said it was going to be a lovely day with only slight breezes. Not sure what the bulge in my pants that was moving around was but I was decidedly not excited. Or so I thought. I reached for my manhood and that's when the scorpion struck my right index finger just below the nail.

The hosannas, hallelujahs and the motherfuckers came screaming from my throat as I danced and jumped out of my shorts and beat them to submission with a broom and an iron skillet. While the scorpion was now dead I had a finger the size of my ankles and a burning that wouldn't let go. I went outside to hose down my finger and try to lance the injection point. I totally forgot I was naked and so when the female deputy sheriff stopped by owing to a complaint from next door I just wanted to climb back in the womb. I retrieved a towel from the outdoor shower stall and put it on. The deputy decided that because I had so much vegetation around it would be difficult to see me disrobed unless someone was really trying and therefore just being a busybody. She looked at my finger and said I should go down to the emergency room. She departed with a grin. I lanced the finger and spent the next hour burning the shit out of myself with rubbing alcohol.

Mo came and got me and had a big laugh about a scorpion taking a nap in my shorts. We drove down to Cudjoe, untied the boat, and went and hid in some mangroves for about two hours. We shared his thermos of coffee and I soaked my swollen finger in a cup of it. By now it looked like one of the units very old men have hanging from their groins in the sauna at the YMCA. Something you want to get away from.

At noon we split for American Shoals having to make contact at exactly two p.m. We set up our phony fishing regalia and turned on the local FM station. I was sure my finger needed amputation. Mo pulled a couple of beers from the cooler and we just sat. Being mid-October it was damn hot and there wasn't any detectable breeze. Somehow sunscreen hadn't been determined to be an essential necessity.

At precisely 1:55 we tossed over a large Styrofoam container sealed with duct tape. Three minutes later the go fast showed up from our south and met us in a very short while. They could easily see the Styrofoam container which contained $75,000 from about a dozen investors. They tossed over 5 large bales wrapped in plastic and half a dozen smaller packages. Many other boats seemed to be converging on the scene. We picked up our packages and proceeded north at a leisurely pace. We saw more packages thrown into the water and also saw many more boats and a convergence of planes and helicopters to our south. Things looked more or less okay.

After a few miles we noticed two separate boats moving in our direction at a very high rate of speed and so we increased ours. My index finger was killing me but my heart was racing at a drastic speed and I wondered if the $15,000 I was being offered was worth it. We came into a group of mangrove islands not far from the overseas highway. One of the boats overtook us almost immediately and just kept going at around 50 knots. That's a bat out of hell on the water. On the aft platform stood a blond girl in a tiny bikini with a mahogany tan. It was an ohmygod moment! She smiled and waved. I waved back. Then she and the boat were gone. The next boat belonged to the Monroe County Sheriff's Department and it was moving only slightly slower and decided we were more catchable at our top end of 22 knots.

The shit was hitting the fan! As we came around the first small mangrove we saw the go fast boat with the chick. It was dead in the water. Captain Maurice saw a passage in the mangrove about the size of a young girl's waist and he took it. The go fast boat with the bronzed beauty took off at full speed and the sheriff followed. I knew we were out of trouble and was about to tell Mo when the boat lurched upward and climbed the trees snapping limbs, our Bimini top and the prop off the motor. I ducked before a large branch took off my head! Several hundred spoonbills who had been nesting on the island took off in a snowstorm of falling feathers and flapping wings. Then, complete quiet.

I got up slowly feeling myself for broken bones and looking for blood. Incredibly I was completely healthy. Captain Maurice was worried that he had killed me. He had not but I still wasn't sure that I wasn't seriously injured. We both took a couple of deep breaths. He had broken half a dozen laws within the jurisdiction of Monroe County, the state of Florida, and a Federal Reservation which owned this particular mangrove. We got on our cell phones and had a friend pick us up. I told Mo that I had absolutely no interest in chain sawing the tree limbs from his borrowed boat and getting arrested for ecological laws after I just beat the floating narco squad. I dispersed in a ghost like way and made for home. Gershwin's entire Rhapsody in Blue played in my head.

Later that week, after I found I actually did have three fractured ribs and needed 16 stitches to my right hip, I once again entered the Parrot. Captain Maurice was there and begrudgingly gave me $15,000 for my troubles. Donna the Buffalo was on the stage and so the crowd piled out onto the sidewalk. One of the Key West boys came by and lit up a doobie. I called Flo and after a few drinks she staggered me to her house where I crashed on her deck on an air cushion. That's the last time I ever fucked around with drugs! It's a fool's game. But, you never know. I certainly check my shorts for arachnids, snakes and rats before I put them on these days. Seems prudent.

WATCHING TOURISTS/TURNING JAPANESE

I was sitting in my car at Fort Zachary State Park, known locally as Fort Zak, reading an old Elmore Leonard novel. If you want to write you should read Leonard's absurd skew on life. Absurdity is where it's at. You can only take so much Hemingway, Balzac (surprisingly I've read all his work) and Twain. If more Twain were available I'd read it. But this isn't a story about literature. It's a story about the dumbasses who come down here and have the need to show to just what degree of a dumbass they can be.

On my second chapter of a story where John Travolta got the leading role in the film, I noticed out of my windshield, some fool girl snapping a photo of a palm tree. A palm tree. Between here and Miami there's about 5 million palm trees. The one in question had no specific personality of note, no characteristics that stood out. It was a fucking palm tree! Whether she was from the Sahara or the great Russian plains I don't know but taking the time and effort to photograph a palm tree was beyond me. Then, only because I cared to notice, she snapped a pic of a coconut on the ground. Oooh. Coconuts! If there's five million palm trees between here and Miami there's gotta be 100 million coconuts that have fallen on the ground. Well, I still had my Elmore.

On the way out of Fort Zak I got stuck behind some tourists on mopeds. Some had girlfriends on the back and some didn't. They were all texting while driving. They weren't driving cars they were driving two wheeled vehicles that demanded they pay attention. That wasn't the worst of it. Some were texting with one hand while consuming a cocktail with the other. It's not even plausible that you can carry a passenger, text, AND consume a cocktail on a dangerous two-wheeled vehicle! Oh, I forgot, its Key West. Dumb fucks! Wait, no, dumb me.

On my first legitimate liberty call overseas in 1973 I went to a bar with a bunch of other sailors with the intent of getting lit up. We were one of six navy ships tied up to the piers in Barcelona. After my very first beer the guy next to me, who had been there for a while, puked up on the bar about two and a half gallons of some purplish substance that needs no further description. The incredibly good looking barmaid showed a face of dismay and called to the Shore Patrol lurking just outside. They carted his ass out of there. Needless to say I wasn't in the mood for dinner. That pales to what I've seen the college crowd do here in March and April. Some of them can ride a moped double, text, drink, and puke all the while driving their vehicles more or less down Duval Street. Not many arrests in that department either.

According to a friend who visited recently you can go to several ATMs and get enough cash to enter a sex club. Upon entrance you pick the mate of your choice and enter a private room. The mate of your choice can be male or female. Once there he/she disrobes and pleases themselves in front of you. You can in turn do likewise. But no touchie, no feelie! That seems like a damn good way to invest $450! For just $425 less you could puke up purplish shit on the bar. And if you're not in the Navy no one gives a rat's ass. This is paradise?

During Fantasy Fest a lot of people of both sexes wear as little as possible. Sometimes nothing at all. A lot of the guys wear banana boats. That's a rig where you place your Johnson in a dugout canoe kind of device for all the world to admire. And there's sure a lot of them. If that wasn't bad enough there's a bunch of people who bring their six year old and their 6 month old in a stroller to watch the attractions. I'm figuring shallow end of the gene pool. Don't bring your kids here unless they're twenty-one! The ladies like to show off too. I had several pics taken of very old women showing their stuff for my camera. I give them credit. It took a lot and after 60 years of stifling Puritanism they decided to let it all hang out. Didn't particularly enjoy it but I had to respect it. Whatever 'IT' was.

When I fish on the bridge some one invariably asks what I'm fishing for.

"Fish," I say.

"What kind?"

"Bull shark," I tell them.

"Aren't they man eaters?"

"Yup."

"Then why are you fishing for them?"

It's not really all that hard to tell someone to go fuck off but with the upbringing and all you do your best. Eventually these dolts will move along. But there's other problems on the bridge. The Cubans always show up with glass beer bottles and find it quite entertaining to smash them all over the road. When they're through with that they take off baby's disposable diaper and just toss it into the water or roll it up and mix it in with the broken glass. As John Prine said, "the whole world smelled like poop. Baby poop. The worst kind"! It gets harder and harder to have my Zen moments out there.

Back in Key Weird young girls are tossing back shots. Nothing straight. Usually some kind of sex on the beach concoction that costs an arm and a leg and little do they know that all that sugar is going to give them the worst hangover their very young lives have ever had to endure. Drink up ladies! And by the way nothing a good looking dude likes better than a drunken 22-year-old puking all over the sidewalk.

Meanwhile back at the beach there's problems a-brewin'. For some reason over the past ten years or so there appears to be a 'large' group of females who think that beach thongs are appropriate in public. The only problem is that these girls aren't the ones you see films of in Rio de Janeiro during Carnival! Being the male pig that I've been told I can be I whimper at the sight of a woman in a thong where not even one little part of the device is even visible. That's because of the cheesecake, kegs of beer, Snickers bars, western omelets, extra syrup, Baily's Irish Cream, peanut butter rum shots, Big Macs with extra cheese, fondue, slippery nipples and anything with tons of butter have been consumed. And since exercise is anathema and "I'm a woman, hear me strong" that will be the future of a certain percentage of the fairer sex. I know a lot of heavier women who hold themselves aloof and dress with quiet dignity. So much so that their shape isn't noticeable. I don't wear tank tops. There's a reason for that. I'm already feeling the gun sights taking aim at me. Not the beach for me. Uh-oh, somebody just upchucked half a ham.

Over the course of the winter when the north is piled high in snow and pipes are freezing in the basement friends will start to come down and visit. I look forward to these visitations. Some Lucky Dawgz will be here, some Connecticut and Rhode Island friends and maybe even my old man, God bless him. I'm sure to have a tequila with Charlie and get to hang out with his gorgeous girlfriend too. The Key West boys and girlfriends are always out and about. Donna the Buffalo will be playing at the Parrot for four days in early January. I've finally got an income to go along with my pension and these bills on my desk will begin to dissipate. Looking forward to cranking up the grill for multiple dinner parties.

I do not look forward to my next trip into town and seeing every person between the ages of twenty and forty texting on their phones while they walk down the sidewalk or ride on their scooters and relay the information that they just peed, pooped, puked or ran into a car or another pedestrian. That's a vacation? I've got plenty to add to this story and I will. After I park my moped, poop and take off my man thong.

TALKING TO OSPREYS

It was another beautiful day on the bridge. The water sparkled with what George Bush called a thousand points of light. That old boy was sure smart compared to his nitwit progeny. What can you do?

Overhead the ospreys were fishing and making a fool of me. I didn't really mind as I had the aforementioned thousand points of light. They have a high register squealing chirp and you know it when you hear it even though you may not see them. In some ways reminds me of the early spring robins in my yard up north while they pull on the warmth-seeking worms just after the winter cold has ended. I have a better relationship with birds than with most people. Doesn't bother me one bit. Funny, though, how they make the same noise.

There's a rough sounding engine noise coming down the road about a mile off. Whoever it is I hope they don't ask about my luck. Tired of it. Get a life. Daddy osprey has a six-inch snapper in its beak and he's heading back to the hundred foot light stanchion with his nest on top. Gotta feed junior. Little guys going to fledge soon. Pelicans glide about an inch off the water. Remind me of World War Two seaplanes. The rattletrap parks at the foot of the bridge and two guys emerge. Damn, if it ain't Joe Beans and apparently some short flunky of his.

Joe glides up the bridge in his old military manner. His buddy waddles and limps.

"Wazzup Jack?" He appears sober, happy and contented. The little guy appears perplexed and disturbed. He smiles showing one of his bicuspids to be missing.

"Nothing up. Just fishing, idling my time. Farting around."

The little guy sticks his right leg up on the bridge railing and takes it off. It's a prosthetic just below the knee. He pulls out a pocketknife and begins to whittle on it. It already has a plethora of artwork that takes my breath away. There's sailing ships, mermaids, marijuana plants, 'mom' and a few cusswords. Joe is talking but I don't hear. The leg is obviously a piece of whalebone or possibly elephant tusk. I'm enthralled. Joe's yakking about something or other but what else is new? That ivory leg is like watching a NASCAR wreck!

"Anyway," says Joe, "I got two bales I pulled out of the drink. You're in for half if you wanna help get rid of it." Shorty is carving up his leg real good. Then the first fish in three months bites the lure. I'm almost dragged into the channel so I know its something big! Overhead three separate flights of F-18s are heading for Boca Chica Naval Air Station. Got the first tarpon on the line in three years and my old pal is talking up a drug deal while the midget is carving on his leg.

For the next twenty minutes I hear or see nothing but the tarpon down in the channel below. I reel in and let off as necessary. Pulling too hard will snap the line. This fishing business takes some patience. Especially if you have a hundred pound fish on the line. I've got more joy than Lucinda Williams when she's singing about Slidell. The midget with the missing tooth makes a long wide swipe at his fake leg and hits my line. Which goes slack. That's the end of my fishing but the beginning of some uncontrollable anger. I go at the little guy but instantaneously there's a knife blade under my chin. I go as limp as my line.

"Put it away Stanley," says Joe. The knife disappears, the little guy backs off, the leg is re-attached at the knee. The mermaid is smirking at me. The osprey swoops low and laughs even though there's a fish in his beak. It WAS a good day and I hope it returns. "You in?" asks Joe.

What the hell! I lost a fish and when is that such a new predicament? I lose fish before I wake up in the morning. I lose fish before I get off of work and get home. I lose fish like I've lost girlfriends over the years so what am I so excited about? The two bales come to mind. That's about $20,000. And damned if the rent ain't due. I look at the squirrely motherfucker with the ivory leg with 'mom' carved on it and relent. "Yeah, I'm interested."

We ended up with about $14,000 from some of my younger friends and it took them 5 days to scrape up the money. The seven grand was a great bonus for me and apparently Stanley was severely anti-drug. Good for him. Good for me. I met Joe at the Parrot and we swilled beers. He shouldn't have been drinking anything due to his overwhelming alcoholism but he could always control himself on beer. It was Johnny Walker and Southern Comfort cohorts had to worry about. A bluegrass band came out on stage just in front of us. Amazingly Stanley was the mandolin player and I have to say he was quite good. He stuck up his fake leg on the counter that separates the stage from the small dance floor. He had two new carvings. One was of a tarpon fighting on a fish line. The other was a carved statement: "Jack's an Asshole."

Later, on my way home, I lit up a doobie and inhaled strongly. The car drove itself home to Sugarloaf. I contemplated the last several days, the tarpon, the pot, and the supposed idiot with the ivory leg. I'm not sure that when we contemplate fame and fortune that you get it this way. Several grand from a discarded bale of grass and notoriety because someone called you an asshole on a prosthetic leg. But, hey, it's Key Weird. Any port in a storm.

I got out my rod and lure and my iced cooler of beer and headed on down to the bridge. A car stopped and the window was rolled down. "Don't even ask," I said. "Don't EVEN ask!"

A LURE, ALLURE

After I got my seven grand from a square grouper deal I set out to buy a boat. Nothing big. Just wanted something that floats with a decent sized horsepower motor. Things didn't go so well initially. As a matter of fact the first boat I saw was at the bottom of a canal and had been there for some time. Guy wanted two thousand.

Pretty ballsy to ask two grand for a sunken boat. As a matter of fact once I saw it and had driven twenty miles for the view I clocked the guy and he too became part of the canal. Float in peace dickhead!

Later I drove down to the Parrot to see who ever they had playing that day for the sound check. Immediately across the room I espied a thirtyish blond siren who hooked eyes with me. Damn, it's been many years since I've hooked eyes with anyone. I put my best bait on the hook and went on over. She played cool, I played cool and she was most alluring in her halter and her shorts. She didn't overdo the makeup and she was very conversational and anyone with a brain could readily determine that she was a lady of some education and finesse. I bought mimosas and we shot the breeze for several hours. Whoever was on stage did their thing but I couldn't begin to say who they were. Mr. Johnson was sending me signals. Funny, at my age Johnson doesn't show up much. I ignored him best as I could.

Her name was Betty and she was a graduate of Yale. She had appeared in Playboy as one of the Girls of Yale sometime back in the eighties. I looked it up later and, yeah, she was hot back then. Pretty hot right now. Johnson keeps letting me know he's around. Man, that guy needs a hobby. We schmooze and talk and laugh and sometimes steal a kiss or two. I have no idea how to get her the 17 miles to my house on Sugarloaf so I don't even try. Maybe she invites me to her place. But I'm not really into that sort of thing anymore. The best part is always the beginning and I want the beginning to last. I tell her about the sunken boat that someone tried to sell me.

She thinks that the deal might actually not be too bad if it isn't holed too bad and the price comes down. She says I probably have to do some apologizing for slugging the seller first. I'm not sure about apologizing to a guy what tried to sell me a junk boat in the bottom of a canal. But she's damn cute and smart and I want the conversation to continue. Apparently in the not too distant future I'm gonna buy me a sunken boat at a bargain basement price. But first me and Mr. Johnson, that pain in the ass, are going to promote our agenda to this here blond siren in the Green Parrot bar!

Things went pretty much the way things are supposed to go. I did my thing. She did her thing. The part we did in two-part harmony was the best. We actually sat up later and smoked cigarettes and chatted about this and that and whatever else came to mind. I didn't want to leave but you can obviously overstay your welcome without being told. I collected my shorts and t-shirt and made a date for the day after next. She threw me a wink. Johnson woke back up. I left two hours later.

I went back to the idiot with the sunken boat and offered him a thousand bucks and a small chunk of my remaining square grouper stash. But he had to raise the boat and accept my apology for the punch. Which he did. But he always kept his distance after.

The boat was not holed. It had sunk in a hurricane about two years previous. Lazy bastard just wouldn't raise it. Now there's a guy that needed a good Johnson. The thousand bucks and the little bit of weed was actually a bargain. He gave one of his buddies a part of the weed and they raised it using whatever means I don't know. It needed a good cleaning from all the sea growth and canal garbage that adhered to it but I didn't mind. I bought a trailer for two hundred bucks and took it home. Damn, I'm gonna be a sailor again.

Cleaning the hull of a boat is hard labor and boring. But hard labor and boring is nothing when you know that Betty is at the end of the rainbow. In between my efforts on the boat I went down to the bridge to fish and consume some beer. It's a beautiful life down on the bridge. Every fantasy this side of hell has wandered through my mind and I was very appreciative. I thought a lot about my summer up in New York and how I would handle that endeavor. The sun shone on the wave tops like millions of tiny candles. Johnson told me to hit the Parrot again tonight. Sadly I was beginning to listen to him. I started thinking religious thoughts. That always killed my sexual desire! I cast the line over and over and thought about old friends and good times and about the relatively short time

I have left. I'm eligible for social security in twelve months and that thought alone I find very depressing. Caught nothing again. So it goes.

Betty and I had dinner at a little kiosk owned by a British woman in a little hideaway just off of Southard Street. The beers were good as were the tacos and guacamole. We headed off down to the Schooner Wharf and listened to a country western band from Oklahoma. We took a walk on the docks and promenade and enjoyed each other's company. We did not enjoy intimacy that night as we were just as glad doing what we had been doing. I went home to my boat and she went home to Massachusetts. She'll be back in three months and probably by then I'll have a boat to show off to her and take her to a private mangrove somewhere and show her stuff she might not know.

Back at the house I've got the boat pretty much in shape after sanding, painting, purchasing of a 200-horsepower Yamaha engine and acquiring all the lines a sea going vehicle needs. I've got a new Bimini top and some used fishing rods and three five-gallon gas tanks. I bought some new fishing lures as I can't stand thawed out stinky smelly bait. I've done everything I can do and tomorrow I'm going out to American Shoals for my very own first fishing trip. I hit the hay and dream very sweet dreams.

The coffee in the morning is magnificent as are the eggs and bacon. I've got my cotton split seam fishing shirt on and a pair of shorts. I've caved in and bought some live bait that's in an aerated bucket. I popped my first Busch at nine a.m. and headed out to the dock. Glorious day with pelicans flying by and not one stinking cloud in the sky. I head to the dock with so much joy in my heart and possibilities in my future. I've finally arrived as a true Key Wester with my own boat with a new engine, a new coat of paint and a jaunty step to my walk. But, where is my boat?

It's at the bottom of the canal. Ten feet down. The phone rings. It's Betty. I pop another one. Wonder if there's an idiot around that would buy a sunken boat?

TAKING A BITE

The road down U.S. route 41 below Fort Myers is quite beautiful, sometimes lonesome and always thrilling. It's the eastern edge of the Everglades otherwise known as the Great Cypress Swamp. There's not a whole lot of vehicles and as a route to Key West its quite fast. That's what Jeremy was thinking when he rode his new $27,000 Harley past the exits to Marco Island.

The first parts of the journey are savannahs and shallow saw grass fields. Then the trees begin to enclose upon you and the highway. It never gets dark or dangerous but there are dangers. Jeremy took in the spoonbills and herons and the rattlesnakes and the alligators in the canal just beside the road. At sixty-five miles per hour life was a joy and there wasn't much traffic to share it with in either direction. The sun was at eleven o'clock along with his watch. The pine tree hammocks off in the distance and the fair weather clouds consumed him in a state of joy. He hit seventy with the wind in his hair and then the world went black!

When the sun shone down on a two lane highway deep in the everglades about a half hour later there was a motorcycle in about three different parts, a very dead and nearly extinct Florida panther, and a man who just woke up to a lot of pain. Jeremy wasn't quite sure where he was but he did know that he was in a world of shit. He could raise his head barely and as he focused he saw that his right leg was quite and severely broken, his left arm was bleeding profusely, and most of the skin was missing from his right. Where his left leg lay, still attached, there were two large alligators with mouths very, very open showing great rows of very sharpened teeth. And just before the darkness returned he heard two separate explosions. As far as Jeremy was concerned the world was over. But it was still a nice day in the Everglades. The type of day you see in postcards!

Jeremy woke up on a gurney in what looked like a person's house. It certainly wasn't a hospital. Working on his legs in a professional manner was a dark skinned woman decked out in hospital scrubs and covered in blood. As he looked at his right leg he saw the dismembered head of a very large alligator attached to it. Boom, boom, out went the lights!

The woman working on Jeremy's leg was a general practitioner and a member of the Miccosukee Tribe of the Everglades. She would have taken a specialty in medical school but her people needed her and the tribe, by way of the local Indian casino, was making money hand over fist. And everyone got a cut. No one needed an oncologist. Everyone needed a local doctor with a little black leather bag full of tools and medicines. There were plenty of oncologists in Miami only forty miles away. She stitched up Jeremy's leg, put salve on his skinned arms and re-set the broken bones. She then attended to his head, which was scraped and bruised and bleeding like a public fountain.

As a Miccosukee Indian Doctor Adrianna Holt was a member of the Seminole Nation, and as such, a recipient of the wealth generated by said casino. The Miccosukee weren't as rich as the Indians that owned the Connecticut casinos but they weren't doing too badly either. Everyone had a four or five bedroom house, two cars, a pickup and an airboat. Her husband, Hog Holt, was the chief of the Western Miccosukee and it was he who unloaded about eight shots from his twelve-gauge shotgun into the alligators that were feeding on Jeremy's legs. At the moment he was in the back yard skinning those very gators for the pelts which would garner about two thousand dollars toward the making of several sets of cowboy boots. With his sharpened blade all he could think of was how the white man lately just kept on giving. He checked in on his wife and Jeremy and then took off in his airboat for a few hours of fishing and/or boa constrictor hunting. His assistant chief, Boris Lavoris, was tinkering with the remains of an expensive Harley Davidson. He was listening to John Prine songs on the local public radio station.

When Jeremy woke up again three days later quite foggy from the influence of massive doses of oxycodone he was looking straight into the eyes of Dr. Adrianna Holt, wife of the chief of the Western Miccosukee. "What the fuck?"

"You were in an accident. And then gators chewed on your toes. You're missing two!"

That was it for Jeremy for another three days. The sun rose in the east. Spoonbills hobbled beside the highway eating bugs and detritus from dead plants. Sparse traffic travelled up and down route 41. Alligators grunted in the dark their sexual calls.

In total cognizance Jerry, as his friends called him, awoke to a beautiful Florida morning. Adrianna brought him coffee and toast. There was a cast on his broken leg and bandages over most of his body. Outside someone was banging on sheet metal but the noise wasn't harmful. Adrianna said that tomorrow he would be practicing on crutches and here, you better take three of these. Boom, boom.

After another week due to questions from Dr. Adrianna Jerry was able to explain that he wasn't married, had no dependents and no one waiting on his return. "How about a job?"

"I was fired. But I don't care. Going to Key West to write a novel." And then Jerry learned to use the toilet with a cast on his leg and a nearly useless right arm. It took some time. But he needed his dignity. It didn't work. Dr. Adrianna did most of the dirty deeds. Days went by and Jeremy got better. Adrianna and Hog were joyous hosts and healing was a wonderful thing except whenever he thought about alligators chewing on his leg.

After a month the cast came off and Jeremy was encouraged to join Hog in his endeavors doing whatever it was that he did. And Jerry thrilled in this excitement and new way of living. Running fast on the airboat, catching boa constrictors and all sorts of fish Jerry was in an element he never knew before. But the limp sure did suck. After a good dinner with his hosts of yellow rice, red snapper, cornbread and collard greens Jeremy decided he needed to get on the road. His hosts presented him with a bill of $3000 for medical attendance. No worries there. Jerry knew a deal when he saw one. Those injuries were worth over a hundred thousand dollars in any general hospital. The time came to go. It was a time to leave a group of wonderful people of the type he'd never met before. He could just cry. The alternative was that a gator would have eaten him.

The next day Boris Lavoris wheeled out a brand new looking Harley Davidson. Jeremy was beside himself. There was no way that bike would ever see the light of day again. Chief Hog explained that Boris was sort of an idiot savant with sheet metal and he didn't want a nickel for repairs. Where do you find people like this? And Andrew Jackson sent most of them running on the Trail of Tears? What an asshole.

After another few days Jeremy took his leave on his almost better than new Harley and presented the Holts with a $10,000 check via his 401k. He thanked them profusely, kissed them both and shook Boris' hand like no tomorrow. Then, he took off.

The road into the keys is beautiful in the early morning. The sun shines in billions of sparkly segments on water of blue-green on both the left and right shores. After a while there is a zone of comfort where your joy is supreme. Until you hit a Key deer at 50 miles per hour which didn't happen because Jeremy was paying extreme attention to all of his surroundings. He had suffered enough injuries. He headed into the main island and parked his bike on Caroline Street. "Are you the president?"

Jeremy hadn't noticed the drunken homeless guy sitting under a nearby tree who had since staggered over to his side. "Are you the president?"

"No, I'm not the president." At which the point the homeless guy clocked him in the nose and actually broke it. Being a city full of police the whole encounter was witnessed by a local cop who was tag teaming with a DEA agent. The drunk was arrested for something like the 15th time. Jeremy was taken to the Lower Keys Medical Center by the narco agent and had a bandage applied to his nose and a compress for his black eye. Not a great day but a hell of a lot better than running into a Florida panther. A little later Jeremy was dropped off on Duval Street and he limped over to the Bull and Whistle. "I'll have a Jack Daniel's, straight up!" What the fuck else could happen he thought to himself. Then a transgender took the next bar seat.

SEPARATE REALMS OF REALITY

Just got out of rehab for the eighteenth time. My hands aren't shaking so much but there is a twitch. The twitch is enough to keep me from the keyboard with my friend Jack's new bright idea. He wants me to write my life story because he deems it to be medicinal and recuperative. For some oddball reason I've agreed as long as Jack does the writing as I dictate. He doesn't like this but he knows there is no other way. I experience sobriety a week at a time only every once in a while. So, it's my way or no way at all. It's not a nice story but if it helps I'll give it a shot. My name is Joseph David Beninsky. My friends and the local sheriff's department call me Joe Beans. Locals have called me many other things.

I have serious psychological problems that local psychiatrists have told me have been written up in the newest DSM. The one thing I know for sure is that I'm not bipolar. I've got about everything else and I ice that cake with a good thick layer of alcohol when it suits me. That and prescription drugs keep me in a low orbit around Saturn. Most people think I'm homeless because I wander the streets drunk and disheveled much of the time. I go without a bath and a shave for many days at a time. I don't enjoy this reality but its one of the two realities I know. After I get out of jail or rehab I sometimes get up to three weeks of crystal clear cognizance. The county calls Jack and he picks me up and we get to converse and hang out for several days. He doesn't try to change me, and, thankfully, he stays in contact with my family and usually whitewashes the facts pertaining to my existence.

I am not homeless. I own a nice conch house on Watson Street and a housekeeping company comes in and cleans it every Friday around noon. They stock the fridge, change the sheets and write down messages from the answering machine so that I will see them on the odd chance I will drop in. Today is one of those odd chances. I have showered and shaved and I have breakfasted on scrambled eggs, toast and bacon thanks to Jack's cooking. He will see to it that I will stay here the next several nights. I am dressed in clean pressed chinos, a bright Hawaiian shirt and sandals. I feel like a million bucks. I actually have four million bucks sitting in 401Ks, savings accounts and investments registered with Goldman Sachs in New York City. My personal bank pays the monthly mortgage and for the cleaning service, electric and water and groceries. I get a $400 cash stipend from a private company on Simonton Street from my investments. I neglect to pick it up on a regular basis. Therefore, when I do, I have several thousand dollars to blow in whatever way I wish and usually I wish to get so fucked up that my maker wouldn't recognize me in a lineup.

Jack says I should talk about the events in my life that have so influenced my de-evolution. Really? Seems like useless shit to me. In my own opinion I am a semi-wealthy lunatic with a reality problem that no one should give a shit about. But I'm sober for the next whatever so here goes. Jack has volunteered to fill in blanks when I am 'somewhere else'. Somewhere else is where I usually am.

In 1967 I was in a Marine recon outfit stationed aboard the USS Iwo Jima cruising off the coast of Viet Nam with 1600 other fast response troops. As a lance corporal I was detached with three other goons to an army outfit working the Ia Drang Valley. Our job was to call in airstrikes from marine fighter-bombers when and because the army had few aircraft for that purpose. We didn't want to hang out with draftees but no one gave us a choice. The North Vietnamese had upwards of two hardcore regular army divisions working the same area. Something like 20,000 of the most disciplined and badass fighters a man was ever likely to run into. The army general running the show on our side was famous for bringing all his boys home. Dead or alive. This is a dear sentiment to the Marine Corps!

The first thing I learned was how to smoke and enjoy pot. I got very good at it and am extremely glad I did considering all the things about to happen. On the third day we were attacked head on in our positions by three platoons of the pith helmeted bastards! I was not in the front line but about a hundred yards back. Still stray shots were taking out soldiers on both sides of me and suddenly the outside of my right upper thigh was on fire. Before I could scream out there was a pith helmet almost in my face who totally disappeared from a volley of shots behind me. That was it, the attack was stopped and I was puking on the ground rattled to the core by the site of another's human insides scattered about me. We had three days of peace after that. There were 40 enemy dead to ten on our side. We had fifty wounded including me. That led to my first purple heart. Until the next attack three days later I smoked two full ounces of pot. Also took several hearty swigs of Jack Daniels that one of the brothers had. I believe I shit my pants.

Jack and I had lived in the same boy's home in a town called Gonzalez in Escambia County, Florida. He was two grades behind me. How we got there is inconsequential and had to do with the juvenile courts. We weren't criminals but no one wanted to take responsibility for us. But it was okay as we got to attend public high school, go out on dates and learn the joys of drinking beer in quart bottles. Not having loving parents was an issue but it was an issue you could deal with considering all the freedoms we had. We had both been in Navy families and both families had been stationed in Key West, Florida in the early sixties. Jack and I lived in the Sigsbee naval housing project on Sigsbee Key and attended Sigsbee elementary. After school every day we went fishing out in the mangroves or we would build plastic model airplanes of World War II vintage and later burn them with lighter fluid to establish the fact that the Japs had just attacked our airfield.

I had three siblings. Two brothers and one sister. My stepfather was often called away on photography missions over Cuba or training exercises in Virginia. My mother, still young, got a little lonely and shared her joys with other men while the old man was gone. He came home one night out of the blue from some secret mission and caught her. In the hallway leading from the four bedrooms he proceeded to beat her mainly to the face and head with his backhand making sure the ring finger made constant contact. The blood was everywhere on the hallway wall and floor. The screaming was loud and sad and very frightening. When the younger siblings awoke and witnessed the carnage they too began to scream and cry and I, shaking like a leaf on an Autumn Aspen felt my first-ever psychological inversion. I was too small to stop it and too afraid to yell or get help. As the blood ran down the walls that dark and very late night the neighbors started to show up and man handle the old man. He ran to his car and drove like a maniac up the Florida Keys into the mainland. The Shore Patrol and State Police were soon on his trail.

My mother was committed to the psychiatric unit at the Navy Hospital. I got to visit her three days later behind a wire mesh window. She was damaged. I was damaged. It was long ago. Then I was sitting in a foxhole, eight years removed, and crapping my pants because the North Vietnamese wanted me out of the Ia Drang Valley! Then the artillery hit. I kissed the bottom of the foxhole and shook during and three hours after the barrage. There was nothing left to soil my underwear with.

Jack and I meet up at the Green Parrot often after I've been released from jail or rehab and have a few beers. Most people would think that alcohol would be the worst thing for me considering my situation but its only beer and Jack never judges. He will not, however, sit or talk with me while I'm under the influence of vodka, gin or Jack Daniels. Good thing as I'm not really there during those situations. He does know that I will not snort coke, shoot heroin or deal in any way with crystal meth. I'd rather keep my teeth no matter how fucked up I feel I need to be. During these meetings he tells me about my grand kids and my brothers and sister. Bless him because I just cannot make the contact. I am a loser in all senses but in some ways I still feel a loyalty to myself.

After a month in the Ia Drang I was recalled to Cam Ran Bay for a little rest and relaxation. Smoked a ton of weed. Drank a gallon of Jack Daniels. During this time I was awarded the aforementioned purple heart and a bronze star because I had called in an air attack under fire after my radioman was shot dead. Don't remember one minute of that action. After that I was sent to a restive spot called Khe San. At least it was peaceful. Smoked a hell of a lot of pot, wrote letters to a lot of friends.

I talked to Jack recently about his stories. I particularly didn't get the one about the talking chicken who served in Viet Nam and settled in Key West after. I told him it took away from any serious consideration he might someday get. He said it was a tribute to the writing of Garcia Marquez whoever the fuck he was. Guess he's got problems too. We're at my house on Watson Street and we're barbecuing steaks and enjoying pink Key West cocktail shrimp with our cold beers. A couple of ladies are coming by and I'm getting excited to talk to a woman while relatively sober. Hope I can keep it together.

****

I'm writing for Joe Beans. After a night of steak, shrimp, beer, some nice ladies and a bag of weed I'm sorry to say Joe took off on one of his tangents. He won't be back for a week. I know where he is but I'm not going looking for him. He is lost in his mind and no cajoling or begging will bring him back until he is good and ready. Joe told me about Khe San. He sat there for two months from November until December in a restive time. They were shelled occasionally but never to any large degree. It was like a summer camp. One day while smoking a joint with some buddies a whole division of North Vietnamese regulars attacked. Bullets flew like random thoughts and grenades landed inside foxholes. Planes and choppers were blown up or set on fire and chaos ensued for the better part of the next 60 days. Re-supply wouldn't even try to land, just toss it off the back of a plane and keep on flying. Joe was shot twice more and personally killed ten of the enemy. He was scared, he was lost and the enemy just kept coming. They attacked morning, noon and night until all civility amongst the marines was lost. They would launch random attacks of their own and destroy and devour and impale everything that wasn't American. Too bad if you were ARVN. It was the deepest part of Dante's Inferno and still things got worse until one day in late February when the enemy simply disappeared. The Tet Offensive had been launched with unmitigated fury and so many died for a cause that no one could figure out. The city of Hue had been demolished. Saigon had street battles and the American embassy was attacked with many casualties. Yet the Americans won the battle. They did however set the stage for losing the war. No less a personality than Walter Cronkite told the American people that their boys were being sacrificed for a worthless cause. Khe San was abandoned and the jungle took over. Joe returned to Cam Ran Bay.

After a month Joe was sent to a small village with his former marine unit of two platoons. One night wandering around aimlessly he found a black marine raping a ten-year-old girl. Joe had a Browning Automatic Rifle and he shot the man's head off. Because of the young girl's trauma he wanted to shoot her too but couldn't make himself do it. After the war through pure Kismet he found out the girl had become a Carmelite nun. Later that night he shot up the HQ shack though luckily killing no one. He was tackled, tied up and sent to the rear. Then he was sent home to a V.A. hospital in Philadelphia. Joe's combat war was over. His personal war had just begun. He was shot up full of restive drugs and left to rot.

Seven days after splitting in the middle of the night I got the call from the sheriff's department. Come pick Joe up. Done it before. Will do it again. Tossed him in the shower and planted him in bed.

Joe had been adopted from the boys home in Gonzalez by a wealthy family in Connecticut. He finished out high school there turning down the opportunity to attend an exclusive boarding school. He had a good couple of years until one day he found out his draft number was 20. He enlisted in the marines. Before he did he made the round of parties associated with his graduation and learned the joys of smoking pot and scantily clad girls. It was the end of his age of innocence. If indeed he ever had one. Joe came home from Viet Nam with three purple hearts, a bronze star with oak leaf clusters, a silver star and the Navy Commendation medal. And a 100% psychiatric disability. After his discharge from Philadelphia he wandered down the eastern seaboard and eventually landed at the end of the road. Key West. I had no idea he was there. I ran into him by pure chance after I had decided to retire there.

****

Yeah, I'm a real live wire. I saw what Jack wrote about me shooting the black guy's head off. I should be pissed about him even mentioning it but this is all supposed to give me clarity or closure or whatever the fuck! And, yeah, I got all those medals but everyone else did too. I wasn't special. I'm still not special. I'm Joe Beninsky, a Polack with no direction. I intend to live this coming week with nothing stronger than a Budweiser going down my gullet. I'm going to hang around home and maybe, just maybe, write my mother a letter. I suppose there is some odd chance for normalcy but I seriously doubt it. I also have come to realize that people love me and I need to take some time to try and return that emotion. I told Jack that I can't do any more of this backtracking this week or the next. But I do promise to continue as the fog and the wood chips in my brain dissipate and lead me to open water. Give me a few days. I suppose I need to explain how I came into four million dollars.

SUNLIGHT

I don't like the word 'remarkable' or its dictionary meaning. Something unusual or worthy of notice. I remark on things all the time. Most certainly are not unusual or worthy of notice. Since I remark on a certain subject I believe that makes it remarkable. I saw, I remarked. People remark on all sorts of things all day long and most of the topics are most unworthy of debate or even thought. With some remarks I get I have to think who gives a rat's ass? Then again I make the same remarks or the same type of remarks. Most are decidedly un-remarkable remarks.

In a song John Prine once made a remark about baby poop. Baby poop was the worst kind he said. I agree. That green shit those little fellers and girls squirt out will sting your eyes, stop up your nostrils, and make your pets hide under the sofa. Baby poop as a topic is remarkable because, of course, it is an unusual subject. According to the dictionary. But, to me, he just made a remark about baby poop. It's a remark and it's remarkable as a remark. Screw the dictionary. Everything is remarkable precisely because you remarked upon it.

According to the geniuses that wrote all the dictionaries found nowadays a remark is not necessarily remarkable. I say if you make a remark it's already in and of itself remarkable. "He's really drunk," I remarked. My companion retorts, "So what, but he really is a remarkable man." He was remarkable when I said he was drunk. That's why I remarked. Anyways.

What's up with this word 'retort'?

And that was the end of Joe Beans' career as a writer with a by-line called 'Sunlight' at the Conch Republican, a Key West newspaper known for its conservative views and values. That the by-line saw the light of day, particularly in that newspaper, was only because of a stacking of unusual events dealing with chance and kismet and just maybe a lunar eclipse. The editor was getting an emergency appendectomy while the assistant editor had to take her dog to the vets after it consumed iguana poop. Possibly the next worst kind a dog could ingest. The publisher was having lunch with George Bush The Lesser on Islamorada discussing the validity of transporting all the Key West homeless, bums, drunks and Democrats to Orlando on the taxpayers' dime.

That left Keith, a former radical and graduate of Columbia school of Journalism, to meet the deadline and print everything fit to print. Having had drinks with Joe in the past at the Parrot he considered Joe to be a genius. Not everyone with an Ivy League education is particularly intelligent. George the Lesser comes to mind. Keith was assistant to the assistant editor and this day was his shining moment. Moment is the key here. His key to the Key, so to speak.

When the editor woke up after surgery and read Sunlight he was heavily medicated. He was so medicated that when his wife reluctantly gave him a copy of the day's paper he laughed so loud at Joe's by-line that he blew out a catheter. Eight hours later he started firing people and it started with Joe. Six people lost their jobs including the head pressman. The union got his job back before he got to his car. Oddly Keith remained on board.

The editor was so staid in his political and religious positions that he still quivered and blushed when he saw a feminine napkin commercial on the television. He saw the first one in 1971 and was seen to squirm and cover his eyes in front of his girlfriend of the time, who was herself, contemplating joining Students for a Democratic Society and was a feminine napkin user. That's what being a Southern Baptist will get you.

Joe Beans couldn't have cared less. He went down to the Parrot about noontime and drank a few pints of cheap domestic beer. He talked to some tourists and some pretty girls who may have been tourists too and almost talked his way into a three way tryst except that his left eyelid began to droop and flutter and scared them away. He paid his tab and made his way to The Bull where the old woman with the loud electric guitar was wrapping her legs around post middle aged male visitors thinking they were being risqué and couldn't wait to tell their buddies back home. Boring!

Joe then bought a pint of Fleishmann's, copped a quarter ounce, and went to visit his friends underneath the Cow Channel Bridge. When asked what kind of day he had by one of his friendly and loyal miscreants he stated simply, "quite remarkable." Unbeknownst to Joe he was the talk of the town for the next several days. A town councilman nominated him for mayor and the police chief mentioned him in a radio interview. Funny what green baby shit can do to you. Funny also what sunlight can do.

Joe had used the title as a metaphor for truth and, unfortunately, the truth had set him free.

4/20

The chair said, "to a good home." I was walking down a small alley after lunch with a friend when I espied the treasonous chair. I sat in it. It spun, it rocked, it lolled back so's you could sleep.

I was of two minds. I was thinking about the Foxhole this coming summer and how glorious it is to see old and new friends conglomerating together while slamming portolet doors and enjoying the sun and view. Hanging out with Alita and Jay and watch the march of the day encompass and envelope me. Thinking back on my time in creative writing classes and listening to Rich Russo of Empire Falls and such and a Pulitzer Prize winner, and thinking, wow, how lucky I got to get his class!

On the first Wednesday all the trucks and crappers are in place. The dumpster sits on the edge of the road. The ice machines are full at the farmhouse. The first folks show up right at sunrise. The sun is starting its elbowing into all our business and the coffee smells like a breakfast cart on Broadway. The ATV cranks up and Jay leads people who are no strangers into a spot they will inhabit for up to seven days. It isn't long before we hear the first beer tabs pop. Toast to you, my friends!

So, I guess its three minds. The chair, the Russo's, the Foxhole.

Long ago the adjunct professor looked on me and said to the class that, "there's a lot to be admired here." Got a hard on. For two minutes. Twenty years later he wins the only prize south of the Nobel in literature. I had made some reference to Emmylou's voice sounding like the noise a pearl makes while sinking to the bottom of a jar of Prell. He told me he was writing a book. Yeah sure. Everybody writing a book. Now you writing a book too. Cynicism put me right where I am.

I took a sit in the swivel rocking chair. Not ripped up, definitely old, but worth a trip up to Lower Sugarloaf. And there its sits like my first 18-year-old conquest, ready for anything and no mother to deal with. Ahh, never happened.

After a while I start re-arranging plants to hang around the chair. I put a glass coffee table next to it and observe from a distance. I should have better, more important things to do but the truth is I do not. Work a lot but those five or six hours after are a blessing and I get to blend with the birds and the fish. I smell better than a fish and even the fish say so. Putting this bar together is a joy but I want a few oddities in design and I want to step back and take a look and maybe decide later as to what I want to do. Foxhole junk jumps into my mind and I have to go down that gravel road and think about it for a while and decide which side I will sleep on come those few hours after sunset. And whether to change my t-shirt.

Most mornings Mik shows up for a coffee or two and maybe a pastry. Some combination of Alita, Jay and myself are at the HQ tent and if Jay is there he is grunting answers to questions. Not a morning person. Alita can be a smartass right off the bat. And boy do I love it! After

Wednesday we have about 30 hours of wonder about where the f**k everyone is. Pop goes the fizzle.

I have to say that after I re-arranged the plants and moved the chair 16 times I'm happy with the result. A good place for a photo op! The mancave is taking on new dimensions as I've got new neon lights from my friend Joe across the canal who is moving to Maine to grow medical marijuana. Not free but cheap. The lights, not the marijuana. Same guy what put me up the top of a mangrove island at 50 mph while driving a boat intoxicated and got pissed because I wouldn't break local, state and federal laws to chain saw him out. Hey, Joe, where you goin' with that gun in your hand? Aside: Delbert McClinton on the radio! Its 84 degrees with a 15-knot wind. Sunny as a California raisin.

I had lunch with Flo at a place that honored our two for one tickets for wine. We were led down the garden path by a twenty four year old Iowan who claimed to know wine like the back of his hand. From Iowa? We were allowed to smoke until the 1:0'clock reservation showed up. They showed up way early and every one of the 70 plus year old women and token grandpa had a lap dog that decided they wanted to lick our feet and eat old discarded chicken bones. They showed disdain when I said the dogs were under MY table. Wished I had a bong to blow in their face. Nothing like a lapdog ordering 8 bags of chips! The building to my left was a dilapidated piece of crap two story probably worth $800,000. The house across the street, equally dilapidated was worth about 1.75 mil. The dogs were attached to the wrong owners.

While driving home with my new swivel rocking chair I thought about the time I was in the room with a Pulitzer Prize winner and all I thought was, "this guy's fulla shit." Sometimes life smacks you in the nose. Sometimes it licks your feet while dining on old chicken bones. Because I have a computer that has a blog created by my friend Malin I get to say all kindsa crap I wouldn't normally say. Sometimes I say it anyway.

Over several days' departure I will have eaten potatoes and onion rings with Rich, had a fish fry with Mike and company, enjoy a wine tasting, watch the sun march across the sky, eat a bunch of gumbo made by the best boys and parents around, drink a bunch of beer, hang with the Vickery's, get bemused by Mark, talk nonsense to Dr. Bob, watch Bonnie bathe, marvel at the Buddha, see my Allen friends, fret over the Health Department, get stupid (it is as does), chat with Flying Pigs, and sleep like a baby!

Up until then I will write a few stories concerning nothing of any consequence and think about my chair, my writing friend, dogs licking my feet and sunrise on July 9th. Shine on crazy diamonds. Then the guy had two movies made. Anybody want to do "Long Black Veil"? Portolets get last hour's beer and last night's dinner ONLY! "Alita!"

RIZ AND HIS RED STRIPE

Riz was having an okay day. Nothing spectacular but at least no bills in the mail or puppies chewing on the corners of coffee tables. It was a good day to walk on down to the Green Parrot and maybe have a conversation with some tourists. The older educated kind that didn't drink till they puked or got loud and obnoxious.

"What'll you have?"

"The usual."

Riz kicked back and took two long swallows of the cold frothy brew. Too bad he couldn't smoke a fatty, he thought. But impossible with the random pee tests at work. I'm in Key friggin' West and I can't even smoke a joint. Key West! Ahhhh! He downed the beer and ordered another. Because of his springtime allergies he sneezed a few times and blew his nose. Then he perused the art on the wall and thought it wacky but kind of low classed. Of course there is a 'no sniveling' rule at the parrot so he let it pass. His sinus dried up rather quickly and of all things a big dry one was forming in his left nostril. He took a peek around the room and swiveled his chair to look outside through the open grated windows. He put his little finger in his nose to extricate the obtrusive article but rather slowly and deliberately so that the unit came out as a whole. This took a lot of his attention. The finger had to go once this way and then another. Nothing like the feeling of grabbing a perfectly formed bugger and removing it in one lump sum.

With finger up nose he reveled in the sun shining big and fat and the sparkling aura of the beautiful day. He daydreamed and had sexual fantasies. He thought of his upcoming cross-country trip. He body checked a New York Islander and scored a touchdown. He drove a new Mustang. He won the Afghanistan war single-handed.

While bugger spearing is a sport to some it is not a totally spectator affair. Unknown to Riz he had swiveled his chair back to the bar while daydreaming and drilling for mucous. Also unknown to him, because he was mentally in five other places the bar had begun to fill up. Over on the other side sat two 20-something Argentinean women with shoulder length brown hair, beautiful teeth and tans to die for. After ordering drinks they sat transfixed at the sight of a man who appeared to have a fist up his nose in some kind of erotic facial sex scene. They weren't exactly grossed out but they couldn't stop watching. Although Riz was a pretty good-looking guy and not built too badly the girls didn't see that. They witnessed a new art form. Others at the bar were also paying attention. Its not every day you can say that you went on vacation to Key West and one of the highlights was of a guy picking his nose. Outside, a drunken bum wearing a t-shirt that said, "I'm Joe Beans and I like red panties" watched through the grates. He took a swig of his half pint of vodka and watched the workout. The bartender backed into a corner and joined the audience.

Randall Mandle was cursed by his name. Seems his parents were sharing several bottles of champagne in the hospital room just after his birth. The tipsy and giggly couple decided on a middle name too. It was Sandle. Randall Sandle Mandle! What a way to start one's life. But the life wasn't so bad. Other than a slight sinus problem in grade school where the teacher had to constantly wipe his nose things went rather swimmingly. Little league, boy scouts, watching the Blue Angels every year at the Naval Air Station in Pensacola and discovering girls didn't have cooties. In junior high his pals began calling him 'RIZM'. Later they shortened it to Riz. Whenever he met someone new he almost always had to recount his birth and nickname changes. Sometimes he would tell people that Riz was the French word for rice. Which was totally true. Then he would enhance the story by saying that the French monarchy worshipped rice or riz so much so that its value was next in line with that of gold. This of course was a wheelbarrow of bullshit and he was always amazed by the people who believed it. He was a great bullshit artist. A bullshit artist with a sinus problem. Needless to say he became a salesman.

The article of his desire was now firmly entrenched in his fingernail and the next step was to remove same slowly. Not aware of anything concerning his surroundings he gently began to pull. Slowly, slowly he pulled and the nugget made its magnificent appearance not only to Riz but to all who sat and stood in attendance. The gem had a comet's tail. This consisted of a wet, rubbery slime that was attached at one end to the bugger and at the other to some dock in a marina somewhere near his frontal occipital lobe. He pulled gently and the flubber extended further and further from his nose to his outwardly extended hand. It looked and hung like a rope bridge spanning across some extreme chasm where Tarzan might be chasing elephant poachers. The audience was enthralled. Some were eating the free Parrot popcorn. The drunken bum outside on the sidewalk yelled, "buggers in my pink panties!" No one paid attention.

With his hand three feet from his nose the rope bridge finally collapsed in his lap. Riz was startled for a second or two but regained his composure and quickly grabbed a bar napkin and cleaned himself up. The bugger was wiped under the bar. The deed was done. Riz looked up and gathered in his visual surroundings. There were perhaps 75 people at the bar standing and sitting and all looking at him. He had just won the world series, the lotto, boffed Marilyn Monroe, suppered with the Kennedys and was awarded a Pulitzer Prize. Best bugger ever!

The quiet in the bar reached proportions equal to that on the moon. From somewhere in the back a single clap. A cluster of college guys were debating whether they had seen this experience in a John Belushi movie. Then another clap and another. Soon a full frontal standing ovation for Riz and his monster bugger. Sometimes you just can't find a hole small enough to climb into. An older fellow with a well-ironed Hawaiian print shirt, whose own daydreams had been assaulted, came over and told Riz he was disgusting. Then he punched him in the nose. The nose. The site of this misadventure. A crimson trickle ran down his face. The new shift change bartender came over with a napkin. "What'll you have?"

The humiliation was immense. Dogging out of there was an option but seemed cowardly. All eyes were upon him. The big old fat sun shone down and the leaves on the trees reflected the vibrancy that filled the air with light on this beautiful spring day.

"Gimme another Red Stripe."

A GOD OUT OF TOUCH

Agnes walked down the upper boulevard tethered to her variably sober male friend. She was short and slim. She was slim because of all the drugs and alcohol she had consumed over the course of a lifetime. She was tanned or one might say burned or even very overcooked. She had scraggly brown gray hair that hosted many species of gnats, bedbugs, chiggers and the like. The hair was oily to the degree of 30 weight motor oil.

Her shorts and blouse were streaked with layers of dirt and mud and grass stains and looked for all the world like they might disintegrate into a mulch pile at any minute. She stunk to high hell! Earlier on this day she had dropped her pants beneath the Cow Channel Bridge to defecate the dinner she had liberated from a garbage can in the back of a local bar/restaurant the night before. In an unfortunate accident she had slipped and fallen into her own excrement and being a water hater decided to just scrape her backside against the concrete foundations to the bridge. Even the iguanas gave her ample walking space.

She looked to be in her late seventies. In fact she was thirty-eight. She left home at 15 and got into crystal meth and heroin. When she couldn't obtain those items she would do any and everything to secure a pint of rotgut vodka. Prostitution is a word that could be used for her activities but she was so cheap to be had the other girls not only disenfranchised her but beat the living shit out of her just for fun. And often. Once Joe Beans told me her story or what he knew of it and I just wanted to cry. But when she walked past I was more concerned with not gagging so bad was the smell. She was lost, oh ever so lost. She held on to the arm of the variably sober man and walked toward old town. The seagulls gave her a wide berth.

Agnes's mind had long ago become defunct. She couldn't communicate verbally but her eyes lit up if you had a bottle. Being a bum cocaine and harder drugs were difficult to come by. Like everyone else in her situation it was vodka or gin. The cheapest variety available. So she drank and she drank and every once in a while she would get ever so hungry and find a garbage can for dinner. Didn't matter how long the garbage had been rotting. She put it away and her body sent a message of thanks or the thanks you get when you know all you're going to get is trash.

Although uncommunicative and listless most of the time Agnes had a wish or some might say a prayer swimming around in the back of her head. Thought processes were slow and the various synapses in the brain usually weren't talking to each other. When she was a youth her and her pals would say something like, "lets get fucked up!" And they did. And she was. Forever and ever. But the wish and the prayer kept swimming around up there waiting for an answer because she was told as a little girl prayers would be answered. All she got every day was a blast of sunshine and oppressive heat. There was no answer. Her whole existence was drink and stink and shuffle along tethered to somebody's arm. She still tried though. Hour to hour she would try to make a thought process that just wouldn't come together. Her prayer was a computer virus. It was a train wreck! No one was hearing.

About 90 galaxies over in an office sat a guy named Larry. Larry was, in fact, God. He and His minions Fred and Jim and Larry junior (Jesus didn't like the Hispanic ring to his name) and a couple of archangels were talking over matters that concerned all the universes. Larry called for a gin and tonic and junior ordered a glass of Merlot. The minions drank cold Busch. You didn't have to be sophisticated to be a minion. Larry made that abundantly clear. During this meeting a deceased and now angelic Navajo code talker came in with some information. He had more or less translated a dream from Earth that he thought had to be acted upon. The minion Fred said, "Man, I was going fishing today. Can't this wait?" The code talker said, "Ah, no." Larry gave a stern look to all in attendance. "Go ahead, Man Who Talks To Fish," for that was his Navajo name.

"I've been looking at these signals for some time now and I believe I have somewhat more or less figured them out."

"Will this mess with Fred's fishing?"

"Yes, I believe it will."

Man Who Talks To Fish then set forth his opinion on what was going through Agnes's mind down on Earth. Junior was a little uneasy and he kept looking at the scars on his hands. Larry said, "Let her rip." And Mr. Fish continued.

"From information I've gathered and collated, with much help from the other code talkers I have found that Agnes, although she can't speak or even think in any understandable method wishes to die and she wishes to die right now."

"Roll the tape," said Larry. And the minions and the bosses saw the whole sordid history of Agnes from birth to the present time with nothing left uncovered. When it was done at least one archangel was seen to shed a few tears. "Approved," said Larry. Junior concurred. The meeting was adjourned but only after junior had spilled and broke his glass of wine.

On Smathers Beach Agnes lay down to stare up at the stars. She was way beyond drunk. The man she was usually tethered to had left her for a vodka party with some other bums. Agnes lay close to the water at low tide. Stinking as she did she found some friends in some land crabs who were more than a little joyous by her presence and her essence. If only she could make sense of her thoughts. If only she could arrange them in some sensible fashion where she might make a prayer that might maybe be answered. The stars were beautiful. How can such beauty exist? she thought. She closed her eyes and remembered being a little girl at Easter. Her mother had bought her a new dress and had given her a bright new Easter basket with lots of candy and checks for twenty dollars from nearby relatives. She searched for eggs in the back yard and giggled when her father tickled her just for fun. It was a grand life. There was no Agnes the drunk, no Agnes the prostitute. There was no Agnes that fell into her own defecation and smelled like the most unholiest shit. The synapses came together for once and decreed blessed mercy unto herself. Larry pulled the plug on his own creation that he somehow had lost and she went into the sleep of oblivion. She was smiling at the stars at the end.

The tide came in and took Agnes. She is now part of the Florida Straits. Sometimes you might see a ring around the moon when you are down in Key West. Some say it's the water molecules doing its prismatic tricks. Others like myself and Joe Beans think that it's a smile delivered by a little girl in her Easter dress that somehow walked into the wrong room.

A NEW KEY

Just returned from trying to get a beer from my cooler. Just returned from where I moved cooler from so that I wouldn't have to make that walk. Oh, yeah, neighbor got me stoned.

He's making a camper out of a brand new 6-horse trailer built for that purpose. Did a great job and now wants to Indian Give on a Blue Moon neon sign he gave me that he wants to decorate said ex-horse camping trailer with. Damn that was a Nobel Prize winning sentence! Against the rules to be stoned. Onward!

By 8 am I was at the beach at Bahia Honda. Cooler stocked and packed with ice. The beach was amassed with the detritus from the Sargasso Sea. It was seaweed upon seaweed. And the garbage, especially the plastic, was strewn amongst the mostly dead growth. Was plenty pissed off. You don't have to toss trash overboard or out the car window! Ever! Drove back home among those driving down for the lobster two-day mini-season. I'm figuring on three different diver related lobster-catching deaths. Spear gun arrow in your cranium? Stayin' in the mancave.

In the mancave I have re-arranged the junk and disposed of much such. There is much more room, a beautiful bar cabinet setup and a new bar with four barstools. To date I'm the only fool who will sit out here in the evenings in 84-degree heat and 110% humidity with a bunch of hungry mosquitos. That's who I am. Bond, James, and so on and so forth. SLAP! SLAP!

I wrote a story recently about Agnes. She represented a lot of people I saw in Key West; it just hits me in the face. If you visit here and don't see the almost two thousand homeless alcoholic bums then you're blind. And the criminal activity they get into? Beyond my capacity to describe and that's what I thought I might do best. Agnes was a thought. Joe Beans was another. I'm going to give it more attempts.

My ex-neighbor who now lives two canals over and owns the six-horse trailer showed me his six-shooter that he keeps in the cab of his truck. He said that when cops stop him and ask if he has a gun he admits and shows his six-shooter. They laugh at it because they have guns that blow out 9 to 13 shots in two seconds. The point being that any gun pointed at a bad guy is gonna make him shit his pants. I may get one. Where the hell is that cooler?

Some of the plants are coming around. I don't know crap about tropical growing but I keep trying. I've tried beans, peas, carrots, watermelons, spices, peppers, tomatoes, and others. Pretty much a loser even with shipped in topsoil and fertilizer. But that's something I don't give in on. I'm determined to make some things grow. To date bananas and tomatoes and green peppers have worked. White flies and weird green worms are my enema and enemy. Getting ready to re-try a cumquat and mango. Timid success with the frangipani. My favorite hobby. And beer helps things along!

Out of the blue I sometimes jump into the canal. It's hotter than bath water and extremely salty. But I get wet and the salt turns my gray hair blondish. Still got vanity. It's like an old bar of soap. My actual shower is an outdoor stall and I've taken every shower here for every day since December 10th of last year. Buncha plants around it so you get privacy. SLAP, SLAP!

I live in a large compound for the Key West area. I thank my landlord profusely for letting me be a part of this. Lower Sugarloaf Key really is a kind of paradise, even with the mosquitos flying off with a part of my thigh. But there are many palms to trim with dead leaves and the new growth seedpods that come in every three months and weigh five pounds apiece. The seagrape leaves need to be raked every week and the Poincianas need to be raked regularly. Then you have to trim back the mangroves and argue with the garbage man to take the shit away. Okay in November, sucks in July.

After all that I'm always looking for a new short story to throw at people. Maybe even later today that could happen. Depends on the beer. Tomorrow I might go down to the Green Parrot and quaff a few. Who knows? For July this rock is crowded as hell and mostly because of the lobster mini-season. I'm gonna try and secure this Blue Moon neon sign and come up with some lies on why its not here anymore.

THE SOUTHPAW

Joe Beans and I were quaffing beers in some nameless dive just off of Duval Street. The rains had departed for a while and the sun shone with immaculate beauty. I kept my eye on Joe to make sure he didn't order a shot of tequila or a quart of Old Grand Dad. He was pretty good with beers. Talkative and coherent.

Out of that bright sunshine walked in a tall handsome black haired guy that looked Brazilian or Argentinean maybe. Joe knew him and they exchanged greetings and eventually introduced us. Georges was indeed Brazilian by birth but had come over as a youth with his parents and settled in mid-Florida. Joe and Georges had served in the marines together in Viet Nam. This all came out as we conversed and downed beer after beer while sometimes commenting amongst ourselves on one or two lovely women that happened to pop in.

Georges not only served in the marines with Joe but had won the Congressional Medal of Honor. He produced it out of his shirt pocket as proof. The bartender, another veteran, plopped us down a couple of rounds of free beers when he overheard the news. Georges told me he produced the medal on purpose from time to time just to get that result. Certainly wasn't shy about it. We shot the shit for about an hour concerning everything and nothing until an AC/DC song came on the jukebox and I insisted we find another watering hole. That pissed Joe Beans off a little but I just can't stand that type of rock music. We headed over to the Bottle Cap for a few more rounds.

After an hour or so I started noticing different guys coming over and saying hello to Georges. These guys were also handsome to an above average degree. Kind of disconcerting that there was some winking going on. But what did I care? Then I noticed Joe slapping down a shot of Cuervo. Oh shit! Then another. I made my apologies and departed the two old buddies so that they could exchange war stories and so that I wouldn't have to carry Joe home. He had been good lately so maybe he deserved a little high time. On this day I didn't have the patience for it. Didn't feel like ending up in the mangroves or Higgs Beach drinking cheap gin with his homeless buddies. I bid good day to he and Georges and went fishing.

About two weeks later I'm having a morning mimosa down at the Schooner Wharf and once again inwardly commenting on the ladies. Georges plops down beside me and says, "Hello, my friend." I greet him in a good-natured way and we chat away about an hour. Oddly, to me, several more guys appear to say hello to Georges and they trade hugs. They speak briefly about things I don't understand but it becomes clear to me that Georges is gay. This understanding does not bother me in the slightest. If you choose to live here you had better get used to that. After the guys leave Georges and I hit another bar on the wharf.

While consuming gin and tonics at an upstairs advantage that looks out over the harbor and all the boats and another beautiful sunny day Georges explains to me that he is a lefty. That's really odd, I think, because he drinks and signs his tabs righty. Oh yeah, I get it. He's

Sandy Koufax in a different league. "Don't worry", he says, "I don't find you attractive." Wow, that was a fastball. Didn't know whether to be relieved or insulted. Then I find I'm thinking too much. "Bartender, a double Cuervo please!"

Not feeling threatened or insulted by me Georges goes into an explanation of himself. It's a long story and sometimes I interrupt to ask questions. He didn't come out until after his Marine Corps hitch. He had his first 'moment' in a high school locker room. He didn't act on impulse but he instinctively knew where his future lay, so to speak. After a while I got up the nerve to ask him if he was afraid of AIDS and other STDs. He assured me that he definitely was and that he took all precautions. After that we steered away from the topic and talked about fishing and cars and even girls. Overall a very nice guy. We would have more beers in the future. I went home thinking of Sandy Koufax and his four no-hitters. Probably the best southpaw of all time. Sidelined by arthritis. Damn!

The next day I find Joe more or less passed out down at the tiny Simonton Street Beach surrounded by bums that know he's got money and probably about to rob him. I even kick one in the crotch, which broke my flip-flop and got me angrier. I drove Joe to his house and tossed him in the shower with his clothes on. I turned the shower water to 'hot.' Then I left. Sometimes it's tough to be his friend. I drove out of town via Truman Avenue and passed the gay and lesbian center near Eisenhower Drive. Out front was an old conch looking much like a Key West bum holding a cardboard sign with a magic marker statement. "Fags are going to hell." To his right, was Georges in a nice pressed

Hawaiian shirt tucked into a pair of new safari shorts. He was holding a sign manufactured by a local media company with beautifully blocked letters and an arrow pointing to his left. The sign said, "Village Idiot!" I laughed all the way out of town.

CITY OF LOST SOULS

A recent picture in my local newspaper shows four homeless men in Mallory Square during the daylight hours. They are showing a magic marker sign on cardboard that says, "Jokes for $2 and all revenues go to alcohol research." Paper actually put this out to the masses.

One of the men was noticed out of state via internet by his family and was induced and cajoled to come home and get his life together and he'd get all the help he needed. When finally contacted he refused because he was having too much fun drinking and bumming and living off the tax payer's dime.

I knew all this on a recent day off when I went to see Joe Beans. Old Joe was sober as a judge. Well, maybe not a Key West judge but a bible-toting Southern Baptist judge from Arkansas. He readily agreed to accompany me on a journey throughout town to talk to some of these people. He knew almost everyone of them and I was already aware of this. Joe was a practicing drunk but he had his own money and a lot of it. At his level of intoxication the only people he could communicate with at times was the homeless alcoholics. He also had me but I'm no role model.

Our first stop was in a cluster of bushes on North Roosevelt Boulevard adjacent to the Marriott Beachside Hotel. Her name was Agnes and little did I know that she had three days left to exist. Her eyes were empty and lacking color. She mumbled a lot and kept picking up and setting down a brown paper sack with nothing in it. Her clothes were so dirty and smelly that I had trouble not gagging. There was nothing in her persona. Nothing! She was attended by an equally dirty and smelly man consuming cheap gin from a bottle. He could talk but mostly he wanted to bum money from us. Joe told me he was waiting on an inheritance from Agnes after she was gone. Couldn't see why he would want more dirty clothes. The bum offered Joe a swig but for once he declined. This stuff depressed him when he was sober. We left.

Our next stop was the bodega on the corner of Caroline and Margaret Streets. In the parking lot next door under a giant Poinciana tree were four or five bums drinking beer in old castaway lawn chairs. They were just as dirty as Agnes. They were yelling obscenities to passersby. Even so a few stopped and gave them uneaten or unfinished sandwiches. Their gratitude was, 'Thanks, asshole!" Mental illness leaked from every one of them like a slow leak on a flattening tire. We walked on down to Duval. It was a beautiful day and countless tourists were doing this and that and trying to take in the island vibe.

Across from the Bull and Whistle we found a homeless drunk sprawled on the sidewalk trying to grab people's legs. He got a few. He also got a couple of kicks in the head. Then he started yelling for the police to protect him because, as a citizen, he had rights that protected him from this dubious behavior. And, he said, he had a good lawyer. If he did I wouldn't be surprised. Lawyers have to eat too. I guess. We took off for the Simonton Street Beach.

Once at Simonton Street Beach I drove down to change out of my painting clothes. I did this as stealthily as possible next to my car door. About a hundred feet away a cop was going through some homeless drunk people's coolers looking for alcohol. And he found it. More cops showed up suddenly and I surmised that in painting clothes and longer hair I looked a LOT like a homeless person myself. I pulled my hair into a ponytail and put on new shorts and a Hawaiian shirt. Then, by God's grace, I got the hell out of there. When Joe Beans and I showed up, there was still a large group of homeless drunks hanging about. I asked the group how they were doing. "Go fuck yourself!" "Got five bucks I can have?" We found my car and split for Higgs Beach. Wasn't noon yet.

At the end of White Street from the condos on the left to the tennis courts on the right, a space of about a quarter mile, we found the Times Square of the homeless. We were in luck. It was the first of the month and every bum with a monthly social security, welfare or disability check was having a big party. These parties lasted about five days until all the money ran out. Then many would find the local psych hospital and explain they were feeling suicidal. Florida law has a special dispensation called the Baker Act. If you or the cops say you're suicidal, the state, county or city has to take you in and decide for themselves if this is true. It almost never is. It's a scam to get a bed, a shower, air conditioning and three meals a day for about five days. How many times can you say you're going to commit suicide via a bungee cord in the local graveyard just to get the spa treatment? Apparently as many times as you like. Joe and I presented us and were immediately given a beer apiece. We accepted.

All the guys including us have their shirts off and were soaking in the sun. It was a college keg party with a weird variation. These were friendly people and they shared what they had. After two apiece we decided to depart, and since the sun was over the yardarm, hit the Bottle Cap lounge. Ahh, air conditioning, beer and the chance to dig into Joe Beans' brain. There was a very cute brunette in there and so my mind went elsewhere. From what I understand from later on Joe left me and returned to Higgs Beach with a fistful of cash. It wasn't anything new. By now my research project had ended with the Brunette. Damn, she had nice eyes!

Two days later I bailed Joe out of the county drunk tank at the local jail. We went to his house and had bacon and eggs and strong mimosas. I read in the paper that a body had been seen floating out on the tide at Smathers Beach but no one had attempted to retrieve it. Joe and I bought some live shrimp and went fishing down to Jack's Bridge. I hooked a very large tarpon but lost it on my light tackle. Not the first time. I thought back on the time when I had buried Dieter the U-boat captain at the end of the road several years before. What a nutty place. What a nutty fucking stupid place. But I love it.

A FART IN THE WIND

Jerry Levine knew a good deal when he saw it. As a stringer for Harper's, Atlantic Monthly and sometimes the New York Times he could submit articles that had a good chance of being published. When times were bad he even submitted to Reader's Digest. This time though he had been contacted by all three of the major publishers who wanted the lowdown of a recently discovered and deceased writer down in Key West. They all wanted 5,000 words minimum. THAT was a big deal. And everyone was willing to pay for expenses up front. Good thing as rooms were upwards of three hundred per night even in the off-season. He went with Atlantic Monthly. Couldn't go wrong there.

But immediately upon researching his topic he found that the deceased author was nothing but a low-life internet-published hack. In his opinion anyway. He got permission for a ten-day stay and that amazed him because he couldn't for the life of him figure out why anyone would want to read the shit put out there by some low life wanna be. He found the blog put out by the dead author and read through his works. "You gotta be shittin' me!" He said it out loud to no one. Oh well, he thought, a free trip to Key West.

A week later Jerry landed at the International Airport and took a drink at the bar. Then he took a taxi to a Bed and Breakfast on Whitehead Street that had been reserved for him. During the flight he had read over the works of the deceased and still couldn't figure out all the buzz. It was pure shit. Good money though and so he went down to where the dead guy used to like to have drinks himself. The Green Parrot. It was early January and the Parrot was hosting a band called Donna the Buffalo. There were so many people crowding into the place and spilling into the street that the police were garnering the crowd from being hit by traffic. Well, this didn't suck and the music, a combination of rock, Zydeco and Grateful Dead, was a treat indeed! Jerry got snuckered and had to ask directions home. A three-block walk to the left with no turns that turned into a 15-block walk with multiple turns. The front desk girl took pity and walked him upstairs and tossed him into bed. He made a sexual advance but in his state she knew he really didn't mean it. She closed the door and he went into a wonderful blissful sleep with beautiful dreams.

When he awoke with a gin hangover, the worst kind, he went almost next door to Kelly's and had a mimosa with a western omelet. He needed to find the former roommates first. They would probably have some good quotes. He already had enough background material to get his article started. He took the $55 taxi ride to Lower Sugarloaf Key and pulled into Hibiscus Lane. Fortunately the Coast Guardsman roommate was there. He explained who he was and why he was there. The Coast Guardsman seemed perplexed. "He was a writer?" He had no idea. The interview took about an hour and all Jerry got was that the author seemed to be a pretty nice 'fella' and, boy, could he drink beer. Not much to put into a story. Jerry went back to his rooms and re-read all of the author's stories. The words were a bit more friendlier this time around, but my

God, why would a magazine put this kind of money into this kind of story? He wanted to talk to Flo, the author's female friend and cohort but she was out of town till Wednesday. He sought the other roommate. He found him at the local community college where he was an adjunct professor of oceanography. "He was a writer?" asked the professor. "He was a nice guy but all he did all day was drink beer." There wasn't much to be had here other than the professor said that the author hated it when he cooked broccoli. Said it stunk like hell! A quote about broccoli. Just great.

Jerry took a day and went fishing on a charter boat. Turns out it was the same boat where one of the author's stories took place. Once the captain figured out who Jerry was and what he was doing he regaled him with the once in a lifetime incident that had taken place on his one time sunken boat. "Shoulda seen those mumblers floating around drunk on their asses, it was a fucking treat. One of the best times I've ever had in my life." Jerry could see that the captain was sincere and had a very special place in his soul for the deceased author. "And think of this, my boat was sunk. All I could do was get drunk and join in the fun. I mean the State Department got involved. There was a movie star, a prostitute and a bunch of Cubans intermingled with these guys trying to get union cards. Funny. Fucking funny. Funny up the ass!" He showed Jerry the place where the boat had sunk in four feet of water. "I'm still laughin', that guy was a lark. So he's dead, huh? Too bad. Helluva nice guy. He could DOWN some beers!" Jerry wrote it all down and recorded a lot on his small recorder. When they got back to the dock the captain refunded him the 400 bucks. "The best day of my life and I'll never forget it." Wow, thought Jerry. Fucking wow.

Jerry hit the Parrot again that night and once again the Buffalo were playing. He had hit some of the big bars on Duval but found them wanting. This place was age correct. He stayed away from the gin. One margarita and two beers. He took the straight-line home and indeed it was only three blocks!

The next day was Thursday so he took it upon himself to interview Flo down on Terry Lane. Although she was home the wooden gate was locked and it took half an hour to find a tenant to open it. He knocked on the door on the second floor. A nice place with a good deck, nice shady trees and tons of ambiance. When Flo answered the door and Jerry explained who he was and what he was doing her jaw dropped to about a level right around her knees. "Jack ain't dead," she said. "He's taking a crap in the back as we speak!"

Well, this was a conundrum! About two minutes later I show up and introduce myself. "You're here to investigate my demise? Hot damn!" Jerry was aghast, stunned and perplexed. He sat in a chair on the deck next to the round table that Flo had fixed up with a late breakfast for her and me. "You're alive?"

I felt myself up. "Apparently so." Jerry looked sick.

After some beer and a few shots of Cuervo Jerry started to settle down. I asked him how he liked my stories. "You suck," he said.

"Yeah but I think being dead makes me better. People love dead authors no matter the talent or lack thereof." He took the tequila bottle and took a very long swig. "You suck," he said again. Yeah, it was a rotten plot to get recognized. "I'm sorry," I said. During instances like this, if there are any, there are long pauses in conversations and plenty of threatening looks. We got over it. We decided to hit the Parrot again for the last night of Donna the Buffalo. After a long talk Jerry and I decided that I would stay dead and he would keep coming out with long lost stories that he had 'discovered.' Worked for me. Worked for him. Damn, I'm the darling of Madison Avenue and I'm still breathing. My friend Charlie and his girlfriend showed up and I tried to explain what was going on. All they heard was Cuervo talking.

The walk home, a trail of maybe two hundred yards turned into a twenty-block stumble with many stops. We ended up in the pool next to Flo's apartment. The caretaker came out and asked what room we were in. "310," I said. "We've only got twenty rooms, pal," so we split. More tequila, more beer.

The next day Jerry was leaving and so he cornered me. "You suck," he said. "You're a fart in the wind."

"But, can I stay dead?"

"Sure, why not?"

Jerry and I shook hands at the Key West airport. You could just tell that the man had had a good time. Jerry is now the editor at the New Yorker. Flo writes her scientific treatises for those who cannot and get paid for doing so. Me? I'm dead. But pulling in a lot of residuals.

A DEPARTURE FROM THE SOUL

I had been awake for several hours but had not ascertained as to where I was. It appeared that I was in a hospital ward and as reality returned ever so slowly I began to make out military uniforms of those upright and walking. There were, of course, many white lab coats amongst the doctors and nurses making the rounds. I heard a conversation to my right apparently among other patients but spoken in German. Then two white-coated nurses came by and rolled me over and stabbed me in the right buttock. No hello. No greeting. Just a shot of knock out juice. And knocked out I became.

Whether it was days or hours later I awoke once again. I had a clear head. I was indeed in a military hospital. In a chair to my left sat a middle-aged bearded fellow. Damned if he didn't seem familiar. "How ya doin', son?"

"Well, I'm hurtin' pretty bad but I'm glad I'm not surrounded by the fires of hell. Who are you and where am I?"

"My friends call me Papa. So you do the same. You're in the Key West Naval Hospital in Key West, Florida!"

"Florida? What the hell?" Then two more white-coated nurses came by and gave me another shot in the ass. Papa was a blur inside of two minutes. I returned from whence I came.

The place I came from was Saipan. I was in the Second Marine Division. I was a lance corporal and I was sitting upright on the beach about an hour after the LCP had dropped my unit off. There was no big battle. Just a few shots by snipers here and there. We all took out our smokes, relaxed, and waited for orders. It was a hot and humid day in the south Pacific and we were all overdressed. As the sweat dripped from every pore from all of us a shot sang out. Then more. It actually did sound like music what with all the different caliber of guns shooting in and those shooting outward. Something stung me in the upper thigh but I was too scared to pay attention. The guy next to me who I didn't even know was shot in the face and died in front of me. I pissed my pants. The other fellows around were starting to fall too. I called for a medic and got one immediately. He was shot in the head and dropped in a heap. I called for another and got one. He was shot in the arm. At that exact moment six or seven Japs came from behind some palm trees and charged us with muzzles flashing. I was stung twice more but I got off some rounds. The newer medic was also hit again and so I just jumped on his body to try and protect him. Another sting. Then there was a bayonet aimed at my heart and I thought of mom. Another marine shot the Jap between the eyes and so the bayonet landed in the fatty part of my other upper thigh.

Another Jap came at me with a bayonet. I shot him in the stomach and he keeled over. I got another sting. I just kept shooting for what I thought was the next two hours. The whole episode lasted less than three minutes. Then everything in front of us was dead. I took a couple of deep breaths and then saw that I was bleeding out very quickly. I tried to scream but found myself swimming in an ocean of deep blue haze. It was oh so nice. I woke up in the Naval Hospital in Key West, Florida.

Due to the many island battles in the Pacific and the ongoing struggles in Europe after D-Day there was an abundance of casualties, especially the wounded. Every Naval hospital, every Veteran's hospital was overloaded with wartime patients. The civilian hospitals were even required in some cases to take the casualties. I never got on a hospital ship. I was loaded onto a PBY seaplane and flown to Guadalcanal. From there I was flown to Australia and then to Hawaii and eventually to San Diego. In 'Dago' the medical generals in charge had to make the choice to disperse patients all over the United States because the Pacific Theatre was only going to create even greater carnage. I was sent to Key West. It took two weeks to get there. I never woke up even once during this transition.

A few days after meeting Papa, having eaten some solid food and being carried to a toilet for a 'dignity' run, my personal doctor came by and ran down the list of things I needed to know. I would be rehabbing both my legs beginning in the morning and would be issued a cane for assistance. The rehab nurses would come for me every day at ten and I would get two hours in the pool. I would walk again and probably wouldn't even have a limp if things went well. I had been shot six times and had two bayonet wounds. One, to the head, I was unaware of, but that explained why I had been unconscious for so long. The doctor told me to check out the nightstand after he left. I thanked him and the nurses came and shot me in the arse! I went back into that comfortable oceanic blue haze.

When I awoke the next morning the two guys speaking German piqued my interest. I asked them who they were. Turns out they were survivors of a U-boat sinking by Navy dive-bombers in the Gulf of Mexico. Several of them had been captured when their rubber boat came up on Sugarloaf Key. One of them had gone to Harvard before the war and spoke perfect Bostonian English complete with the accent. They professed their loyalty to Germany but they were not Nazis. Then they spoke of their friend and shipmate, Dieter, whom they knew had gotten away and would surely never be caught. Later that day a bunch of MPs came and hauled them away. Not Nazis eh? Sure.

I never took a look on my nightstand until Papa came back. Damned if he didn't look familiar! He took a seat next to me and told me about his efforts to hunt submarines in the gulf aboard his fishing boat. He had a Tommy gun and a box of hand grenades. Grenades against a submarine? That's like throwing pebbles against a water heater. He agreed. Then he directed my attention to the nightstand. He picked up an article that was anchored at the bottom by some shiny metal. It was hung from a necklace type device. It had five stars on it. It was foreign to me as I had never seen one and had never conversed with anyone about it. "What is it," I asked.

"The Medal of Honor!"

I didn't see Papa again for two weeks or so. Maybe he was out hunting submarines or something. I did, however, learn from my doctor that the gentleman was a Mr. Hemingway. He was an extraordinarily famous writer and journalist and had just returned from Europe, where word had it he was the first American in Paris. The doctor, however, seemed unimpressed. He told me that he and Papa had shared drinks on occasion, and that the current swollen left eye of his was due to a punch from same. He then saluted me on winning The Medal!

At the end of those two weeks I could walk with a cane and was given liberty. I was required to wear a dress uniform and I was also required to wear my medal or medals as it turned out. I also had a bronze star with oak leaf clusters and a purple heart with six stars. I was kind of proud but it looked so much show off and unnecessary. But, damn, I would do anything for a cold beer! After I dressed in my clown outfit with all the medals Papa appeared from nowhere and said he was taking me downtown. Here I was laden in jewelry and picked up by one of America's most literary famous heroes. Sure, I can do that. He had a beat up old Buick and we drove downtown to Captain Tony's Bar.

As we walked in about five in the afternoon I heard clapping and cheers and I wondered who just got married. As we headed indoors I saw all these people at the bar and in the dancing areas giving a standing ovation. It occurred to me suddenly that this was for me. After five minutes or so everything soothed out. The proprietor, a friend of Papa's asked what I'd like to drink. "A cold draft beer and a shot of tequila," I said. More cheers. Of that evening I can't remember much. Only that I thought at one point where that large tree growing out of the bar was going to end up. I didn't get back to the hospital that night. I ended up on Whitehead Street at Papa's house. In a king sized bed with satin sheets!

The next morning with a hangover that felt like road graders going through my brain a foot with six toes gently pulled on my covers. Then a couple more showed up. I'm allergic to cats. I sneezed my way downstairs. After finally finding the kitchen Papa was there to greet me. Even though he had out drunk me at every juncture the night previous he looked like a Greek god ready to pounce upon the heathens. Clara, his black housekeeper and cook was making scrambled eggs and grits. "How ya doin', Jim?"

"Its James."

"Right Jim, and I'm Ernie. NOT!"

I was dressed in a pair of cut-off jeans and a t-shirt. I had no idea where my uniform and medals went until I spied them hanging on a kitchen cabinet door newly cleaned and pressed. "We're going fishing, Jim. Already called the hospital. You're cleared."

So we went fishing. We went down to the Turtle Kraals where his boat was temporarily docked and loaded up with live and dead bait. Some MPs came by and gave him another case of hand grenades. Seems he had some pull. And off we went on the Pilar, named after his last ex-wife. At times while we were underway he would get quiet and seemed to be having some inner conversations with himself or his demons. He held on to the helm like it was his lifeblood. I chanced to ask him what he was thinking about so hard. "A giant fish," he said. "And an old guy that's trying to catch him." I wondered if he was talking about himself. We caught several marlin that day. It was incredible fun but the strain on my injured legs was a bit too much. He noticed my grimaces and we headed back to shore a little earlier than he would have liked.

Over the next several weeks he took me back to Captain Tony's, showed me some drinks I never heard of and showed me how to clock some guy who might be causing trouble. One night a guy and a girl came into Captain Tony's and I stood transfixed staring at the girl's behind. It was a great behind. Unfortunately her husband didn't take to my admiration and a situation arose. Papa came over and got between us. "Hey, pardner, that guy there has won this country's greatest award and has done things you'll never know about." I was in full uniform per requirements of the time. My medals were in full view. I found it embarrassing actually. Don't see myself as a braggart. "If he wants to stare at your girl's ass just let it be. He ain't acting on it." The guy made to reply but Papa just clocked him. Knocked him on his ass!

After a month of waking up to six toed cats the Navy Department sent me on a war bonds tour. It was December and very nice in the keys. I didn't want to leave but duty called and I wasn't given the slightest choice. I had a few last cold beers with Papa and Captain Tony on a Thursday evening. "If you ever need anything Jim, just let me know." I gave my thanks and walked out the door and got on the Navy shuttle bus. I never saw the man again.

I did however keep up on his works. We traded a few postcards but his notes held an edge of sadness. Many years later I saw what he did to himself in Ketchum, Idaho. I hoped that he had gotten to clock somebody in a local bar before that last breath he took.

I got married and had three sons. All in all I was happy with the family I had created. Then one day my wife died of breast cancer. My oldest son, a marine, died in the Ia Drang Valley while attached to an army unit. My youngest died of a heroin overdose while protesting outside the Democratic Nation Convention in Chicago in 1968.

My middle son also served in the Ia Drang Valley but went on and got several degrees in literature and journalism from some very classy universities in the east. He actually wrote this story. I don't have it in me. But he had no poetic license. He took down every word I said and printed it. He didn't edit. He didn't criticize. I love him. I moved back to Key West at almost 70 years of age. I saw Captain Tony before he died and he remembered me. I had a draft beer and a shot of tequila with him. When I left I retrieved my cane, which was certainly a requirement these days. As I departed a blond guitar player guy was singing about getting wasted away again. A tree was growing through the roof of the bar. I decided to walk up Whitehead.

MARGARITAS ALL AROUND

I met Joe Beans down at Higgs Beach. He was making frozen drinks for all the local bums and having a helluva time doing so. I took one also. It was a bright and beautiful Key West summer day. Plenty hot but a day with great expectations. Joe had a generator and was pumping out drinks electrically like nobody's business. He was also giving out five-dollar bills to everyone who took a drink. If they came back for another they got one more five-dollar bill.

Joe did have a prerequisite to his charity. You had to take a dive in the ocean to mitigate the body stink. Some of the bums took pause with that but he held steadfast. No bath, no drink. And no money! Suddenly there were a lot of clean Key West bums. A little salty but clean. Joe called me over and he made me see how happy he was. It was like pouring beer at a college keg party back in the seventies. If you were the pourer you were the man! After an hour or so he picked up his gear and we stowed it in my car's trunk. Then we headed off to the docks at the end of Margaret Street.

At one of the local bars we settled in and had a few beers. Joe wanted to talk. You could just feel it. Apparently today was the anniversary of his father's death. It was okay for me to listen as Joe on beer was better than Joe on vodka or Joe on tequila. Because that was when he became a hopeless homeless himself. We were safe. "Did I ever tell you about my father's war record?"

"No, I don't think you did."

"He was a hero in dubya dubya two."

"No shit."

"Yeah, he was a character."

"Like you?"

"Way beyond me dude."

"What did I tell you about calling me dude?"

"Oh yeah, sorry."

"So tell me."

And he did so.

Joe's father had been shot multiple times during the invasion of Saipan. His two brothers and his mother were dead. His father had about two months to go. The problem was that Joe and his father didn't get along any more. They liked each other but Joe's habits didn't fit well with his father's old-time mores. Joe had written his father's biography and it had been published. That had been done twenty years previous and the work had had some acclaim. They shared some monies but Joe took off, leaving his job as a professor of American Literature at one of the more well-known Connecticut colleges and ended up as a pseudo bum in the Florida keys. Where he drank himself into a sort of oblivion for a few years. That's where I met up with him again. I had to clean him up and sober him up and surprise upon surprise Joe had a nice little conch house all paid for and cleaned by a maid service. I had actually been there before but it was always a new shock to see how well he actually could live if he chose to do so.

Joe's father had won the Medal of Honor during his short service time. One of the many benefits entailed for this singular achievement was that his kids could attend a service academy for free. Joe selected Annapolis and graduated with honors. As a second lieutenant of infantry he was sent to Viet Nam in about two minutes. Considering his brother had been killed in the Ia Drang Valley the year previous he wasn't very thrilled with the posting. When he read through the rules of engagement he wondered what in the fuck was his government into. But there was a lot of booze and a bonanza of drugs. He partook of both. Heavily.

We cooked up some steaks with onions and broke open a bottle of pinot noir. We decided to hit the Tiki Bar over on my island and Joe could sleep in the hammock in the mancave. It was trivia night at the Tiki and I aced the first round. As usual I was enthralled with the bartender's ass. What can I say? I'm an ass man. Some younger blond chick sat down next to me while Joe was exploring the place. It became entirely obvious to me and the rest of the bar that she was a hooker. I figured it out when she told me about all the places on Duval Street where she had danced and been fired. She didn't look too bad and had a nice tight black body skirt. But she was pimply. She had the kind of pimples you see on people who just don't bathe much. She didn't have any kind of over powering stench but I certainly didn't find her attractive. We conversed a little and very soon she threw a monetary amount at me. Fifty bucks. Wow! Fifty bucks is immediate drug money. Nothing more to it. If you're young and semi-attractive in the Florida keys you should be demanding at least several hundred.

Joe came back around and I ascertained that he'd had several shots of tequila. Can't hide that smell. But he was a happy doofus and he caught on to the hooker's gig immediately and went about teasing her about all the things he would like to but never would do. The hooker couldn't pay for her drink and we didn't volunteer. The barmaid with the nice ass kicked her out. The minions of people that I barely know came by after and said they had even money that I would leave with the girl. They were shocked that I didn't. But they also seemed friendlier than usual. It was respect. Can't say I hadn't thought of it in the far past but I'd like to die with my unit intact. As I told my new admirers, "that's why God invented masturbation!"

Joe and I headed off to my house about a mile away. We sat in the mancave with the neon bar lights I had purchased from a guy who had gotten sick of his surroundings. The same guy who drove me up into a mangrove island on his boat at 50 miles per hour nearly decapitating me. We got rescued by the same guy that had even money on me and the prostitute. Joe found my tequila and took a good long swig out of the bottle. "Geez, you've put in a lot of work here," he said. "Looks like some of them joints just off of Duval." It could have been a compliment. It could have been a disparaging remark. I took the bottle and had my own good long pull. I wasn't driving anywhere. Joe passed out in the hammock and I went upstairs to watch the weather channel. Just before the first hurricane alert of the season I passed into a heavenly air conditioned sleep and dreamed of shooting hookers disguised as metal ducks down at the penny arcade. I vaguely remember passing the gun to Opie just before Andy showed up and discovered the barrel was bent.

At around 4 am I awoke and headed for the kitchen. I found the blender and made a batch of frozen margaritas and then I woke Joe up. He was plenty pissed until I stuck a frozen drink under his chin. We went out on the dock and watched the space shuttle fly by to the northeast.

"Wanna hear a story?" he said. "Yeah, sure."

He pulled a joint out of his shirt pocket and lit it up. He took a long satisfying hit and passed it over to me. "Well, one day a long time ago..."

JOE TAKES A LITTLE TRIP

If there was one thing I never expected it was seeing Joe not under the influence of some sort of liquor. But when the bartender down at Don's outdoor bar called me up and explained a few things I knew I had to beat a path to that locale and check up on things. I split from Flo's place on her girl's bicycle, happy for once that a certain kind of injury just couldn't happen. I took the long route and passed the gay/lesbian center where the redneck was disparaging faggots and the gay guy was disparaging the former's lack of logic. I was thinking those guys should take that show on the road. There was a music fest in Rhode Island that could probably use them for filler between acts.

I could immediately see that Joe was under the influence. And it wasn't from alcohol. Firstly it was a cloudy day and he was in the shade with sunglasses on. Wasn't a criminal act but strange for him. He would squint all day long in the sun before he allowed himself that white stripe of untanned skin around his eyes. Not vanity. Just Joe stuff.

I pulled up a barstool and ordered a Busch. "Wanna tell me what's going on?"

"Ooga booga," he said.

Oh brother. I ordered a double shot of tequila. I took his sunglasses off and looked into his eyes. Pupils as big as Palm Island! He began trying to catch imaginary somethings out of the air. The bartender who had called me said that this had been going on for several hours. In all that time he had taken two sips of his small draft beer. He had put a dollar bill on the bar every fifteen minutes or so and had created an equilibrium between him and the management. But the bartender thought that the call was necessary. He was quite correct.

"Uh, Joe, just what the fuck are you doing?"

"Take a little trip, take a little trip with me. War, 1972."

"Joe, you're a drunk, not an acid head. Why?"

He looked me dead in the eye and said, "Chickens." I downed the tequila, chased it and ordered another beer.

"I talked to a rooster yesterday. Set me straight. You have no idea what's going on." No, I didn't, and at that point I thought it would make better sense to bicycle back to the gay/lesbian center and listen to the debate.

"I met Henry junior and after you've met Henry junior your life is forever changed. Did you know chickens are people too?" Man, he was too far gone. Hey barkeep get me another. Joe's beer looked like tepid bath water. He took a tiny sip. "Who knew?" he said. "Who knew?"

"I'm gonna tell you a story and you have to sit there and listen. Yeah, I'm tripping. Haven't tripped in 25 years. But yesterday a rooster walked up to me and started to talk. At first I thought I needed the psych hospital. If a chicken talks to you then there must be a serious problem upstairs." You see these crazy bastards all over the place? They're fucking nuts. They talk to people who aren't there. They have conversations with empty rooms." For a wild man he seemed curiously cognizant. I listened.

The bartender winked.

"This chicken, name of Henry, accosted me just around the corner yesterday. I wasn't drunk. Didn't have any tremors. I turned a corner and there was this rooster smoking a big fat Cuban cigar. Did it look strange? You betchyerass! The only smokin' chicken I ever saw was on a spit. There's no logic to this I know. And I know I'm fucked up. And I know you think I'm crazier than those bums that hang out at Higgs Beach!"

Then Joe told me the story. He sounded as sober as a southern Baptist judge. My jaw dropped as he went on. I suddenly wished that I had a hit of acid. Way too long in the tooth to do so but the story was in another realm. I did, however, have a good bartender and so ordered some new drinks, clearing out the toilet water Joe was drinking. Myself and the bartender lent our ears to an incredible story told by a famously drunk Key Wester about the Sad Demise of Henry! A hen and her chicks were pawing in the ground outside for grubs and cast off human detritus. A jet landed at the airport. This weird place got even stranger!

I WALK THESE STREETS

When my son was twelve and almost 13 years old I sat him down for a talk. I told him he could use the family lawn mower to go into business for himself. He had to have a spreadsheet to show his profits and taxes he would have to pay. He went into business and made me extremely proud.

I loved this guy more than the world. My wife and I doted on his every need except when he got to the point where he thought our offers were things he required. When he got full of himself.

One day I went down a list of things that would piss me off if he partook. At almost thirteen he couldn't help but to wise off one night. Whatever he said caused me to give him an open hand slap. Very hard! I didn't draw blood but I knew that the slap hurt. We got over it. Time just passed by. We fished, we shopped, we did father and son stuff. Then, one day he was eighteen. He got drafted three days out of high school. Those fucking politicians! I never saw my son again.

On another day my son, a U.S. Marine, was guarding the embassy in Saigon. It was 1975 and everyone with an American connection, whether a passport, a tête-à-tête, or some investment in the stock market got on the roof of the American Embassy and tried to fly off. My son, the marine, was standing by the gate with loaded M-16, when a Viet Cong with a grenade in his underwear decided to blow himself up. The letter we got from the Defense Department did not mention this. We got this from his friends. I believe he was the last American casualty. Two months later my wife died. She just expired. No cancer, no leukemia. Just dead!

I ended up in Key West. I wasn't a bum and I wasn't homeless. I got myself a place and then just decided to stare at the sky day after day. And day after day I remembered the day I had slapped my son. I had no reason. As King Tut, the front of the family, I took it upon myself that this was my job.

Then I ran into Agnes. She was a partying little girl with huge issues. I tried to be her friend. She was going nowhere. She drank a lot and did huge amounts of drugs. I knew her perhaps two years. Then she went into another realm where I seldom saw her and if I did she was one lost lassie! One day she died. Read it in the paper. I had some kind of adoption in my mind. I thought maybe I could care for her and make her right. I was a dozen years too late. Early one day she drifted out into the Florida straits.

I drifted off into some place where everyday started with me slapping my son. The little wise ass who was only trying to tell me that he had gotten to a place where he could think for himself and that some of my adult decisions were pretty lame. I laid a hand on this beautiful son, my progeny, who gave me so much joy. My guilt is boundless. It grows in length like the Russian plains. I pulled the pin from the grenade. To blame it on a sadly wayward wannabe communist doesn't relieve me of the shame. That's why I'm here at the end of the road. Because I can't go any further. I walk these streets and wish that so many things weren't so. I walk these streets and see the joy and agony of each and every face. And in each and every face I see my son.

THREE THINGS YOU DON T SAY

Walking down these weird streets is a pure joy with Flo. Especially after polishing off a bottle of Pinot Noir with our steaks. We aren't staggering yet, we may have another drink somewhere, but just kind of grooving on the tourists right now. Bunches of 'em. Thick as flies!

One corner we almost never frequent is Greene and Duval. Everyone wants to hang out at Sloppy Joe's, pretending they're communicating with Hemingway and taking lots of pictures on their cell phones. Flo and I have the chuckles. It wasn't just the wine. Then we ran into a guy with a talking parrot.

The parrot, like most parrots, did not have a huge vocabulary. He or she said a few silly sentences and the crowd was supposed to laugh and offer money into a five-gallon bucket at the owner's feet. The first thing the parrot said when I was milling around was, "I fucked your mom!" Then he said it three more times. Money flew into the bucket.

Now, wait a minute. A parrot just said he fucked my mom? This is legal? This is right? Of course the physical enterprise involving this feathered fiend and my mom wasn't possible. Nor was the telling of such deed ethical in my mind. Flo looked at me worriedly. She had plenty to worry about. I sent her on her way and she didn't argue.

Caught sight of her heading into Captain Tony's. "You taught the bird to say this?"

"Yeah, sure, champ. Got a problem with it?"

Well, yeah, a little one. The roundhouse from my right hand began somewhere around my right buttock. It gained speed and momentum around my right chest. It landed furiously on the jerk's nose, which satisfyingly broke upon impact. I'm sad to say that the force of the punch continued onward to the parrot sitting on the jerk's right shoulder. It died before the asshole's nose started bleeding. Died before it hit the ground. The tourists, tanked as they were, got all out of hand nervous and screaming and creating quite the scene. I saw two cops on the beat heading my way. I sat on the curb and awaited my arrest. Thankfully I had the bail in my pocket.

Key West is still Key Weird. I didn't clean up the town. I did pay for a nose repair. My record was eventually expunged. If you ever get a parrot don't teach it stupid sentences that may offend someone. I'm sure the bit about wanting crackers and such is getting old. Try this: tell your parrot that daddy just got a set of Goodyear E-78/14s and his traction has never been better. That would be a clever parrot. A parrot with a long life.

MURDER, MAYHEM, AND MARIJUANA

Walking down these extremely hot streets during the summer I get to notice corners and locations where a murder or a stabbing might have happened not so long ago. I remember the murders. I remember the mayhem. Some people just get so blitzed out of their minds that they find a secret highway and ruin their lives.

Some fella a few years ago beat the living shit out of a gay guy because he was gay. He's serving life in prison and rightfully so. But if you've ever seen a sidewalk fight on Duval then you've seen a full-length feature movie. Fists, broken beer bottles, women screaming and lots of blood. And the meanest police you've ever seen!

The coconut telegraph contacted me one day and told me about the marijuana floating up on Smathers Beach in separate shrink wrapped packages. Well, hell, I had an hour to play before the law might show up. No one calls the police on the coconut telegraph. Found a thirty-gallon garbage bag and headed to town. There wasn't even a crowd yet!

I found twenty 'bricks' of pot. Weighed a ton. It was a 15-minute investment. Threw it in the car and scrammed. When I got home I unpacked everything from its plastic and I surmised about two kilos of extremely waftable Columbian weed. Paranoid as I was I re-packed everything in triple-layered plastic bags and buried the total haul in the back yard. Then some time went by. Then some more.

One day it was three years later and I still hadn't found or even approached anyone in an open discussion about how to disperse of said detritus buried below the ground.

However, as time went by, my neighbor's dog, the Jack Russell named Cooper, started doing weird stunts on top of my mancave bar. Sometimes he would bark furiously at cats that just weren't there. A few times he did a complete three hundred and sixty degree backflip! One time he took a John Grisham novel off the bookrack and brought it onto the bar. He opened it to page 27 and started to read. At least that's what I thought I saw. I opened the tequila bottle on that one. Didn't offer Cooper a drink. He took off after an iguana and caught him. Did things to him that honest pets should just never do. Who am I? I murdered a parrot! But one less iguana meant one more tomato on my tomato plant in the morning.

At about the same time I noticed a hole had been dug in my yard. A hole where I had buried the marijuana. It hit me all of a sudden why a dog should be doing backflips and reading John Grisham novels. I dug all the remainder up and put exactly one ounce in a baggie. I took the rest and dumped it into the canal. That should help the new coral polyps to grow! It was late Saturday. The Prairie Home Companion was on the radio. Pretty close to heaven for me. Cooper shows back up with a Carl Hiaasen book in his mouth. Hardcover. $24.99! I swear he's got iguana blood on his mouth.

That night needed to end. It didn't end right there because I hit the little plastic baggie. I also read Cooper a chapter out of the Hiassen book. Never saw a dog so much in need of wine and cheese. I turned the lights off and went to Havana. Me and Papa were drinking gin and tonics. He comes around now and again.

The next morning I got the coffee maker going and waited around for my reward. I poured a cup and went out to the dock on the canal. When I arrived a huge red snapper was hangin' on the dock with a gill leaning to one side. He was wearing a pair of circular sunglasses like Janis Joplin on the cover of one of her albums. He had a red solo cup that looked like it had a bloody mary in it. "Hey Bud," he said. "Got any Worcestershire sauce?"

THE SECOND TIME AROUND

A married couple, friends of mine from Albany, told me once that on guitar you have to let the refrain or the place where the lead is played go around twice. I didn't know this. Afraid I fucked up a lot of jams until that point. I thought my 15 chords gave me a license.

But I'm willing to learn. They taught me a lot. I even let things go around four times just to be safe. Especially if I wasn't singing. Those were boring songs.

But as to other things in life I see where things should really go around twice...or more. I'm not singing harmony with Bank of America. I think they only know the 'E' and 'A' chords. Pretty good Buddy Holly stuff. But they ain't singin' my tune. Most presidents go around twice. You learn their song. Except Jimmy Carter. A wonderfully crafted human being was kept out of the White House for a second term because of where he fell in history. Iran's internal politics elected our next president. And that man went around twice.

My brother, the one with the same last name, wants me to come up to Sarasota to his ranch and beat the hell out of a coupla Les Pauls for a night. Complete with Marshall amps, cold beer and a big bag of weed. He won't go around twice because he never learned that. AND he only knows six chords that I can distinguish. Likes noise though. Just as I did at 22 years. But my brother is 56! I'm thinking heart failure, hilarity and the county sheriff! Not saying it's out of the question. I first met him when he was 18 years old and full of shit. Signed a co-sign for his motorcycle. The same bike Peter Fonda rode in Easy Rider. My brother, wearing only jeans with no shirt and no underwear got into an accident. Fairly serious. Whether fortunate or not the first person to my brother on the ground was a twenty-year-old hottie who showed all kinds of concern. Unfortunately my brother's jeans ripped at the crotch and his unit just stuck out there. He had some broken bones so there was nothing he could do. As the sirens were already singing he asked her to leave and she did. She didn't come back. She didn't come around twice.

I did though, and he's one boneheaded motherfucker. Can't help but like him. During a weekend soon I'm going to show him how to go through a song part twice. I don't know the technical reference of such. This will be my second time around with him this year. He has the old amps with the tubes in them. Best amps ever invented! It'll be good as long as I don't have to hear 'Smoke on the Water' or '25 or six to four!'

I think I'll just tell him that you need two times around so you can get excited all over again.

AVOIDING TERRORISTS

I was cleaning up palm fronds from around the yard. They were getting quite away from me. And when you consider that picking them up means you have to participate in the weather or in my case the metal smelter, well then, its an unpleasant task. Very.

Cooper the terrier comes around looking for his treat. I tell him I'm looking for a little more progress in the iguana eradication program but he doesn't understand. Here, take your friggin' treat and bolt! That's what he does. He's chasing a pelican. Good luck with that.

At that moment a mini-Cooper pulls into the driveway. It's Joe Beans in his new car. Wasn't expecting him up here this far from Weirdville but I was very glad I had filled and iced the cooler. Cooper (the dog, not the car) came around to bark his protests. Cooper (the car, not the dog) blew its horn and goodbye doggie!

"What up, Dude"?

"I told you I prefer asshole to 'Dude' any day of the week".

"Yeah, where's the fun in that"?

"Screw you. Beer?"

"Hey, its me dumbass!"

That settled that. I was surprised as hell that he would drive the 17 and a half miles to see me. And although the car was rumored in previous conversations it was a bit unnerving to finally see. Joe Beans growing up. What was he, 55 years old? We shot the shit and had a couple brews. Then he decided to help me around the yard. That was grand as the different varieties of palm fronds sometimes needed to be cut up to fit in the trashcans. We had to lay off the beer in the sun and neither of us was bothered. Water does some very good things for the body. After three hours we gave up and jumped in the canal. The mid-September water temp was about five degrees cooler than August. It was actually soothing.

I pulled some steaks out of the freezer to thaw and put some briquettes in the grill. Joe wire-brushed the grill top and we went after the cold ones again.

"What brings you up here? You never leave that rock. By the way you're staying in that hammock tonight. No choice. You're doing it"!

"Thanks, appreciate it. Afraid that almost every bum in town now knows I have money. And that sucks".

"Getting leaned on, huh"?

"Leaned on? Jesus Christ!"

Then Joe told me about every hard luck case in the keys wanting to borrow or needed 'front' money for various enterprises. Not one of these enterprises involved leaving the island and starting a better life. I knew Joe had a monetary worth exceeding four million dollars several years ago. It was probably higher now. The problem was that every single bum for the next four islands now knew it too!

"I've got people wanting me to buy them houseboats. Can you believe that? And they want me to stock them with booze!"

"You need to get off the island."

"Yeah."

We worked on the grill, got the meat out and made a tossed salad. Around five we put the steaks on the grill. The F-18s out of Boca Chica roared overhead. Some landing. Some leaving. A thirtyish blond lady with a Playboy body walked by in pasties and a string. We were very quiet. But she saw us anyway and came into the man cave underneath the house. Joe, not a bad looking guy and still in relatively good shape, took the lead in the conversation and was soon heading to my room. Motherfucker! I tended to the grill and just daydreamed all sortsa weird shit. Motherfucker!

In half an hour they came back down. She was flushed and made her apologies. She wouldn't be staying for dinner. Joe had a smirk on his face like some 20-year-old. I told him that he knew where the clean linen was and the washing machine and detergent and he had better get to it! He took to his duties with the same smirk. Jerk!

After dinner he told me about all the money terrorists that were after him and some who said they were going to hurt him if he didn't deliver. After all the time he had spent with them and given of his deep pockets. "Buncha shits," he said. "Buncha shits."

We went down to the Tiki Bar and played trivia for about two hours after dinner. And after my linen was cleaned, folded and replaced. We watched the sun go down off beyond Key West and won a few drink rounds at the game. He's quite the intelligent guy. He only drank beer and I didn't see him sneaking tequila even once. We found some people to shoot the breeze with and a few hours melted into pleasantness. We headed back to the man cave and shared some more beer.

"I can't have all these people chasing me around for money," he said. "They don't even try!"

"That sucks. But I thought you shoulda dumped them all years ago."

"Well, they're terrorists, pure and simple. If they don't get what they want they threaten me. Maybe I'm through with them."

"That would be a GREAT move!"

We had a few more and listened to the news on the radio. An Islamic group in Iraq was having a field day chopping off American and British heads. Bad people doing bad things. We talked about that for a while. Then Cooper (the dog, not the car), came by for a treat. Funny little guy. We tossed him one end of a rope and he grabbed it and snarled for fifteen minutes. Joe said he wanted to think alone for a while. I suggested the bridge just down the road. He knew it well and its medicinal values. He jumped into his Cooper (the car, not the dog) and took off. I sat around for a while and just thought about the meanness of people. The world can sometimes suck. Bums wanting free rides. Jihadists cutting off heads.

Joe came back an hour later. He pulled the Cooper (the car, not the dog) into the driveway. He opened the door and Cooper (the dog, not the car) jumped out. The girl with the pasties now dressed in white shorts and a respectable tank top appeared in the man cave once again. She was quite nice and there were no more shenanigans. The two Coopers fell asleep in the driveway. We all chatted very nicely about nice things and things we'd all done in the past. At some point I went upstairs to sleep. Joe wasn't drinking hard liquor and he wasn't threatening to drive his car. I left him and the girl alone. He told me later that he had not discussed his financial background and he had walked her home two streets over. When he came back to my house he was accompanied by Cooper (the dog, not the car).

GRAVEYARD IN THE MANGROVES

I was in the sixth day of my cleanup. It only took a few hours each day and the progress gave me great satisfaction. This was to be my other man cave, but the one with total and absolute privacy. A place where a generator and a laptop and some beer on ice might show me some inner creativity. A place where I didn't have to speak with people.

This was Dieter's old camp. He was a U-boat captain during World War II. His boat was sunk by navy dive-bombers and he ended up here in these mangroves. He survived to a ripe old age and I had met him several years ago. I also buried him. He had told me some great stories. His rescue of a family of shipwrecked Cubans was the stuff of low-level legend. You only heard about it every once in a while usually in one of the watering holes frequented by locals. Although spoken of well in these missives he was known as the 'Nazi Captain.' I knew this aspect to be incorrect. He had told me his story. But now, with my new hideaway, I said nothing of it during my infrequent visits to the Tiki Bar.

On the seventh day I had a generator and refrigerator hooked up and had brought in a bunch of 5-gallon gasoline containers. Dieter had plenty of extension cords stored neatly in a shed. As a matter of fact his encampment was a joy of organization and common sense. His main shack had a waterproof roof. His food storage cabinets still held food not contaminated by the elements. There was enough Spam, tuna and pasta that could be eaten for the next ten years. But I brought more. Then I drove down to the bridge to fish for ideas.

The old Zen master in the sky wasn't cooperating today so I developed a plan on only coming to the camp by bicycle. The car on the side of the road in the middle of a mangrove swamp was going to stick out. So I went home and put a couple of baskets on my bike. Threw in a loaf of bread and some mayonnaise and returned to camp. It was getting dark so I lit some mosquito smoke and a few candles. Pulled up a lawn chair to the brightest candle and whipped out some Hemingway. Why not?

There was the slightest crunch of shoes on coral. I looked up and there was Max, the agency man. A friend but one scary motherfucker! Wasn't sure that I hadn't soiled myself. I'm totally hidden in the jungle so the surprise was complete.

"Howdy Jack." He wasn't in a lighthearted mood. Sweat dropped with anger from his brows and saturated his shirt.

"Hi Max," like seeing him was nothing out of the ordinary. "I know you're not here for the free accommodations. How in the world did you find me here? Wait, never mind, I wouldn't understand anyway."

"Joe's in the hospital. Stabbed in the gut and both wrists slashed. Lost a lot of blood. Someone gave me a call. All I know is that Joe isn't suicidal. Usually drunk as hell but he wouldn't off himself." I did not know. He went on to tell me what he knew and that he had flown down from Knoxville. The fact that Joe Beans was hurt very badly began to set in. Joe, Max, and I were pretty good friends. We'd all met in a holding barracks long ago waiting for our discharges. We got along, chased women and drank too much. We went our separate ways but always stayed in touch. Max, in his dark world, had worked out of Key West several times and he always made contact. Beers at the Parrot or dinner down at the A&B.

"Is he gonna be okay?" I prayed for a good response.

"Affirmative son. Probably ten days in the hospital then back to normal or his normal."

"Aw, shit, that's great!" The pressure in my chest let off a bit.

"But, I know who did it and that man is gonna pay."

I avoided that particular realm of the conversation. My insides were in turmoil. "Where's the beer?" I pointed. The guy finds me in the middle of a fucking mangrove swamp totally removed from all civilization and can't find the beer. Come on! Probably a rhetorical question. After some small talk we hiked out of the swamp and about a mile down the road where Max's car was parked at a boat ramp. Cuban teenagers were busily littering the nearby bridge with beer bottles and cardboard bait containers. I didn't have the time or energy to toss choice adjectives at them.

At the hospital we were led to Joe's bed in intensive care. He looked a mess with all the bandages and tubes but he was sitting up and smiling at us. The nurse gave us ten minutes. We did not know that Joe had been injected a few minutes earlier with a knock out shot. He smiled at us in a goofy way, drooped his eyelids, and was gone. The nurse gave us a sarcastic grin. The Lower Keys Medical Center and its satellite organizations have some of the meanest people in the South. Max with one of his secret devices cut the back of her blouse from top to bottom and she never knew. Until we got to the unit exit door and offered our own bit of sarcasm with silly waves bye-bye. She stood in the aisle naked from neck to waist obviously mentally kicking herself for not putting on a brassiere that morning and wondering about her garment malfunction. Nice rack for a mean little ass wipe!

Max just disappeared. I didn't need to think about what he was doing. I knew a little of his reputation but we usually steered clear of what he did for a living. I stayed at Joe's house over on Watson Street. Just a few days later I got a call from the hospital to come pick up Joe Beans. He was signing out against doctor's orders. The man, the legend! I picked him up in his new mini-Cooper at the Emergency entrance. He was attended in his wheelchair by Ms. wiseass. She wouldn't look me in the eye.

After we got back to Joe's house we discussed him coming to the mangroves.

"Its a very comfortable place, Joe. Absolutely no distractions."

"Isn't that where Allis Chalmers used to hang out with the Nazi?"

"One and the same."

Well, lets pack up some clothes and food and do it. I need out of this society for a while." We did just that after changing the dressings on his wrists. The stitches were mean looking, the skin like undercooked hamburger.

I later found out that Max had cornered his man. His street name was 'Smut.' Joe had been charitable to this bum in the extreme over the last several years. But Smut wanted the treasure chest and when he saw Joe staggering in a darkened section of Caroline Street he went after him. He threw him on the ground while repeatedly kicking him and then rifled through all his pockets. He got nothing! In a rage he stabbed Joe in the stomach and then slit both wrists. He was a former locked up psychiatric patient that Florida was not allowed to keep locked up forever. Max' informant saw the whole thing and called the ambulance. Then got the police stationed at the corner of Duval. Then he called Max.

Max had followed his information like a bloodhound. In the salt ponds area behind the airport he found his man drunk but coherent.

"Ah, Mr. Smut I believe!"

"Who the fuck are you cowboy? Hey, can you spare a sawbuck, haven't eaten in two days?" The little camp was almost totally empty excepting one other drunk passed out underneath a boxwood tree. He wasn't moving any time soon. Max took out a pistol from one of his pockets and sat on a plastic milk crate. Smut was digging through some old cardboard boxes for who knows what. When he turned to make another plea for money Max shot him in the left knee. The gun report made almost no noise but the screaming Smut could be heard at the Marriott nearly a mile away. Could have been heard except for the United Airlines jet just then taking off.

Smut rolled around on the ground screaming bloody murder. And there was a lot of blood! Max tossed him the dirtiest old rag he could find from the camp's trash pile. He started counting to himself. It was early morning and he new the schedule. After three, two, and one the American Airlines jet reached crescendo noise just above them. Max shot Smut in the other knee. Old Smut was in a world of pain!

"Like robbing your old pals and benefactors, do ya? You DO know what I'm talking about, right? Pretty good with a knife too I see. Why not get a job at Benihana?" The suddenly not quite so psychotic bum, assaulter and street thief began to beg for mercy.

"Don't kill me, man!"

"Never crossed my mind." Max once again began counting to himself. Three minutes later the early morning pontoon plane to the Tortugas flew over. A shot rang out and Smut lost the first two toes from his right foot. He was given more filthy rags. Smut was rolling around on the ground in the worst kind of agony. Max told him he hoped they would never meet again. Then he kicked him square in the jaw, which broke in two places. On his way out of the salt ponds he called an ambulance. It was only fair. The call was untraceable.

Max returned to the mangroves to visit with Joe and I. He asked for a shovel and a pickax. Then he went over towards Dieter's grave and began digging a hole. He went at it for three hours never letting up. That coral is tough digging and it takes a lot out of you. When he was done he came over to the old picnic table and sat with Joe and I for a while. We had a few beers but I put a limit on Joe because of his medications. "What's the hole for?" asked Joe.

"Don't worry, its reserved." We had no idea at the time that Smut was under the weather. I read about it next day in the papers. Oddly the police chief didn't think the event warranted investigation. It was criminals hurting other criminals. In actuality Max' connections in the 20 various law enforcement agencies assigned to Key West was all it took. A little verbal arm-twisting. Besides, Smut was paying far worse than if the police had gotten involved.

Max said his goodbyes to Joe and I and disappeared into the black hole where he resides. Over the next several days Joe got much better. I called his sometime romantic interest and brought her out to the swamp. I left him some beer but removed all traces of hard liquor. As he told me later it was the best romantic getaway he had ever taken. During those days the moon came up majestic and full under cloudless skies. Tropical breezes told stories to the bending palm fronds. Small waves lapped at the foundations of The Bridge, which for some reason or other was immaculately clean and free from the dimwits determined to destroy it. Joe Beans is a very good man.

Thank you for reading.
Please review this book. Reviews help others find
Absolutely Amazing eBooks and inspire us to keep
providing these marvelous tales.

If you would like to be put on our email list to receive
updates on new releases, contests, and promotions, please
go to AbsolutelyAmazingEbooks.com and sign up.

About the Author

Jack Mazur studied creative writing at Southern Connecticut State University in the 1980s under Richard Russo, who would go on to win the Pulitzer for *Empire Falls* in 2005 or so.

ABSOLUTELY AMAZING eBOOKS

AbsolutelyAmazingEbooks.com
or AA-eBooks.com

27608452R00175

Made in the USA
Middletown, DE
19 December 2015